LUCENT LIBRARY *of* HISTORICAL ERAS

RELIGIOUS BELIEFS IN COLONIAL AMERICA

RELIGIOUS BELIEFS IN COLONIAL AMERICA

DON NARDO

LUCENT BOOKS

A part of Gale, Cengage Learning

GALE
CENGAGE Learning™

Detroit • New York • San Francisco • New Haven, Conn • Waterville, Maine • London

LIBRARY OF CONGRESS CATALOGING-IN-PUBLICATION DATA

Nardo, Don, 1947–
   Religious beliefs in colonial America / by Don Nardo.
      p. cm. -- (The Lucent library of historical eras)
   Includes bibliographical references and index.
   ISBN 978-1-4205-0266-4 (hardcover)
   1. United States--Religion--To 1800--Juvenile literature. I. Title.
   BL2525.N355 2010
   200.973'09032--dc22

2009051204

Lucent Books
27500 Drake Rd.
Farmington Hills, MI 48331

ISBN-13: 978-1-4205-0266-4
ISBN-10: 1-4205-0266-2

Printed in the United States of America
1 2 3 4 5 6 7 14 13 12 11 10

Printed by Bang Printing, Brainerd, MN, 1st Ptg., 06/2010

Contents

Foreword

Looking back from the vantage point of the present, history can be viewed as a myriad of intertwining roads paved by human events. Some paths stand out—broad highways whose mileposts, even from a distance of centuries, are clear. The events that propelled the rise to power of Germany's Third Reich, its role in World War II, and its eventual demise, for example, are well defined and documented.

Other roads are less distinct, their route sometimes hidden from view. Modern legislatures may have developed from old tribal councils, for example, but the links between them are indistinct in places, open to discussion and interpretation.

The architecture of civilization—law, religion, art, science, and government—as well as the more everyday aspects of our culture—what we eat, what we wear—all developed along the historical roads and byways. In that progression can be traced every facet of modern life.

A broad look back along these roads reveals that many paths—though of vastly different character—seem to converge at a few critical junctions. These intersections are those great historical eras that echo over the long, steady course of human history, extending beyond the past and into the present.

These epic periods of time are the focus of Historical Eras. They shine through the mists of history like beacons, illuminated by a burst of creativity that propels events forward—so bright that we, from thousands of years away, can clearly see the chain of events leading to the present.

Each Historical Eras consists of a set of books that highlight various aspects of these major eras. For example, the Elizabethan England library features volumes on Queen Elizabeth I and her court, Elizabethan theater, the great playwrights, and everyday life in Elizabethan London.

The mini-library approach allows for the division of each era into its most significant and most interesting parts and the exploration of those parts in depth. Also, social and cultural trends as well as illustrative documents and eyewitness accounts can be prominently featured in individual volumes.

Historical Eras presents a wealth of information to young readers. The lively narrative, fully documented primary and secondary source quotations, maps, photographs, sidebars, and annotated bibliographies serve as launching points for class discussion and further research.

In studying the great historical eras, students also develop a better understanding of our own times. What we learn from the past and how we apply it in the present may shape the future and may determine whether our era will be a guiding light to those traveling future roads.

Introduction

FROM RELIGIOUS FREEDOM TO RELIGIOUS TOLERANCE

The summer of 1656 was a troubling one in Boston, hub of the Massachusetts Bay Colony, which had been established twenty-six years before. The colony's founders and citizens were Puritans, religious fundamentalists who believed that all people were born sinners and must constantly prove themselves to God through demonstrations of piety. When unsure of what God wanted of people, they looked to the Bible and to their ministers, whom they viewed as the chief interpreters of God's will.

The Puritans drew a sharp line between themselves and another Christian group, then called the Children of the Light, or the Quakers. (Their later official name—the Religious Society of Friends—did not develop until the 1700s.) The Quakers had recently broken away from English Puritanism. So they held most of the same beliefs the Puritans did. The main difference was that Quakers believed a small spark of God's grace resides in every person. So there was no need for intermediaries (priests or ministers) between people and God, nor for baptism or other symbolic rituals.

These differences may seem trivial today. But in the 1600s they were seen as huge, especially by the strict and zealous Puritans. That summer of 1656 two young Quaker women, Mary Fisher and Ann Austin, arrived in Boston on a ship from another English colony, Barbados. When word of the women's presence spread, the assistant governor confined them to the ship. On his order, Mary's books were burned, and she and Ann were thrown into the local jail. The authorities made it known that any person who so much as spoke to either prisoner would be severely fined. Then they stripped the women naked and closely examined them for signs of witchcraft. For five weeks the two languished in a filthy, pitch-black cell and then were placed on a ship and sent back to Barbados.

This was not the last persecution of Quakers in Massachusetts. Two years later the colony passed a law mandating the death penalty for the return of any Quaker who had been previously banished from the colony. Soon after that, several more Quakers were discovered in the Boston area. One, an elderly man

Quaker Mary Dyer is led to execution in Massachusetts Bay Colony. Dyer was hanged for repeatedly visiting the area despite being banned.

named William Brend, was beaten brutally, receiving 117 lashes with a tarred rope. A local official justified the punishment, saying, "He endeavored to beat the [religious laws] black and blue, and it was but just to beat *him* black and blue."[1] In the two years that followed, Massachusetts went further and executed three Quakers, including a woman, by hanging.

The Roots of Intolerance

The religious intolerance demonstrated in these incidents in Massachusetts in the 1650s was not at all unusual at the time. Numerous people in the early decades of the English North American colonies were punished and persecuted for their religious views and practices. This appears strange to many people today, partly because of misleading statements made by a number of early modern teachers and textbooks. A common claim was that the Puritans, Pilgrims, and several other European religious groups came to the Americas seeking religious toleration. The reality was that they sought religious *freedom*, not toleration. Louis B. Wright, a noted scholar of colonial times, writes:

Let no one imagine, as school children have sometimes been taught to believe, that our ancestors came in search of "religious toleration." Toleration was a concept that few of them recognized or approved. What they wanted was freedom from interference by opposing religious sects or unfriendly official authorities. Once firmly in the saddle themselves, sects that had been persecuted in England became equally zealous to root out heretics [people with dissenting beliefs] from their own order.[2]

It is only natural to wonder about the source of this fervent, sometimes fanatical intolerance. Where did such fear and hatred of differing religious views and opinions in early America come from? The answer is that the initial settlers brought these biases with them from Europe, where religious hatred and divisions, including among various Christian groups, were then quite common. In fact, one cannot properly appreciate the development of religion in colonial America without an understanding of the peculiar religious situation in Europe in that era.

The chief religious antagonists in Europe in the 1500s and 1600s were the Catholics and Protestants. Both worshipped the same god, considered Jesus Christ divine, and venerated the Bible. Yet Protestants had recently broken away from the Catholic Church, viewing it as corrupt. They had come to see the words of the Bible as the central authority in all religious situations and disputes. Catholics, by contrast, viewed many later-established church rules, along with the authority of the popes, as equal in importance to the Bible.

This and a few other differences between the two groups may seem fairly small today. But in early colonial times they were a source of intense hatred,

An illustration of the St. Bartholomew's Day Massacre, in which Catholic soldiers attacked and killed Protestants in Paris in 1572.

brutal massacres, and even full-scale wars between Protestants and Catholics. Some Catholic countries, including Spain and France, tried to get rid of their Protestants by deporting them. But many Protestants bravely resisted. Eight separate religious wars occurred between 1562 and 1589 in France alone. People on both sides committed horrible atrocities. One Protestant, for instance, repeatedly killed Catholic priests, cut off their ears, and made them into a neck-lace that he wore every day. A Frenchman of the era writes:

> Barbarous cruelties were committed by both sides. When the [Protestant] is master, he ruins the [Catholic religious] images and demolishes the [Catholic] tombs. On the other hand, the Catholic kills, murders, and drowns all those whom he knows to be of [the Protestant] sect, until the river overflows with them.[3]

In retrospect the most notorious example of such bloodshed born of intolerance was the St. Bartholomew's Day Massacre. On August 24, 1572, a Christian holiday honoring St. Bartholomew, Catholic soldiers attacked Protestants in Paris, slaughtering men, women, and children without mercy. Similar massacres took place in other French cities. And in all, more than seventy thousand Protestants were slain in only a few days. Their main "crime" had been their refusal to recognize the pope as their spiritual leader.

Even more horrendous was the Thirty Years' War (1618–1648). Largely a religious conflict between Catholics and Protestants, it ravaged Europe during the very period in which America's Plymouth, Massachusetts Bay, and Jamestown colonies were in their formative stages. Germany, Denmark, Sweden, France, Spain, and other countries were drawn into the war, the most savage conflict Europe had ever experienced up to that time. Thousands of towns and villages were reduced to rubble, enormous tracts of farmland were destroyed, and at least seven million people died in the fighting or of disease.

A Unique and Powerful Combination

To escape this sort of extreme religious intolerance, various European groups struck out for North America in the 1600s. Many, like the Puritans, were happy to be free to worship as they pleased. But once they had settled in America, they were no less intolerant of other faiths than many European faiths had been of them.

Over time, however, a wide diversity of groups settled along America's eastern seaboard. In addition to Puritans and Quakers, there were Anglicans, Lutherans, Catholics, and numerous other Christian denominations. Also in the mix were Jews and African slaves, as well as the Native Americans who inhabited the continent when the whites arrived. The beliefs of these people were as diverse as they were. And that very diversity forced a new and different attitude toward religion, one never seen before, to steadily develop in the colonies.

Indeed, it is a testament to the greatness of the civilization that grew up in colonial America that what had begun as religious freedom without tolerance steadily evolved into a state of both freedom *and* tolerance. This unique and powerful combination was adopted by the founding fathers of the new nation that united the colonies in 1776. Thanks to the long and sometimes turbulent religious experiments of colonial times, that exceptional mixture of religious freedom and tolerance became enshrined in the founding documents of the United States. Perhaps none of these writings describes it more eloquently than the Virginia Statute for Religious Freedom, written by Thomas Jefferson and adopted by the state of Virginia in 1786. It states:

> Men have [long] assumed dominion over the faith of others, setting

up their own opinions and modes of thinking as the only true and infallible, and as such endeavoring to impose them on others. . . . [This shall not prevail in Virginia, where] no man shall be compelled to frequent or support any religious worship, place, or ministry whatsoever, nor shall be enforced, restrained, molested, or burdened in his body or goods, nor shall otherwise suffer on account of his religious opinions or belief, but [instead] all men shall be free to profess, and by argument to maintain, their opinions in matters of religion.[4]

Chapter One

Native American Religious Beliefs

When white Europeans began settling the eastern coast of North America in the 1600s, they encountered a host of different Native American, or Indian, peoples. Although these native groups shared some cultural traits, ideas, and practices, they were more different than they were alike. They spoke hundreds of different languages. And they had diverse lifestyles and customs, including numerous different ways of obtaining food and building houses.

The Native Americans also differed tremendously in religious beliefs and practices, the European newcomers found. One expert observer describes it this way:

> Indian religion presents a wondrous variety of beliefs, sacraments, and systems. Different tribes or re-lated groups of peoples had different views of the supernatural world, with varying types of deities and spirits . . . ghosts, or the spirits of dead ancestors; animal and plant spirits; spirits of natural phenomena, such as sun or rain gods; benevolent or guardian spirits . . . and malevolent [evil] demons. . . . Along with these diverse types of supernatural beings, Indian peoples had [differing] mythologies and lore concerning the creation and structure of the universe; an array of rites, ceremonies, and sacred objects; and differing systems of religious organization.[5]

Like Christianity and other faiths the Europeans brought with them, Indian religions had certain uses that benefited and/or met the needs of their societies.

Most dealt in some way with the concept of an afterlife and ways for people to prepare for it. Also like most Old World faiths, Native American belief systems provided nonscientific explanations of the world, universe, and natural phenomena; tried to predict the future through omens (divine signs); strove, through prayer and sacrifice, for victory in war; and gave both communities and the individuals who lived in them emotional stability, hope, and peace of mind in an often confusing, unpredictable, and brutal world.

Unfortunately for the Indians, most Europeans did not recognize these similarities between the faiths that had developed on opposite sides of the ocean. Most of the newcomers came to view Native Americans as inferior and savage. And calling their beliefs primitive and childish, the Europeans frequently tried to convert Native Americans to Christianity. Such

Most Europeans who arrived in North America did not understand Native American religious beliefs and attempted to convert Native Americans to Christianity.

Native Americans saw a spiritual quality and meaning in the earth, plants, sky, and animals.

intolerance and lack of respect led not only to hatred and bloodshed, but also to the disappearance of many native belief systems.

A Few Shared Concepts

In addition to the wholesale loss of many Indian religious belief systems, a number of others changed over time because of the disruption of native cultures caused by white expansion and settlement. The overall result of these trends is that it is difficult to reconstruct accurately many of the original Indian faiths. But fortunately, varying amounts of information about some of these faiths have survived. And this has allowed scholars, both Indian and non-Indian, to draw some general conclusions and make some educated guesses about Native American religion in colonial times.

First, these experts say, although there were hundreds of different Indian belief systems, all, or nearly all, shared a few basic concepts. For instance, these systems saw no substantial difference between the natural and supernatural worlds. According to University of Delaware historian Christine Leigh Heyrman:

> Native Americans perceived the "material" and "spiritual" as a unified realm of being—a kind of extended kinship network. In their view, plants, animals and humans partook of divinity through their close connection with "guardian spirits," a myriad of "supernatural" entities

who imbued [filled] their "natural" kin with life and power. By contrast, Protestant and Catholic traditions were more inclined to emphasize the gulf that separated the pure, spiritual beings in heaven—God, the angels, and saints—from sinful men and women mired in a profane world filled with temptation and evil.[6]

Another quality that most or all Indian religions had in common was that they were all-embracing rather than compartmentalized. The majority of European faiths tended to view or categorize religion as only one of several major aspects of society or a person's life. Other aspects included marriage, one's occupation, the local government, and so on. And there were a number of days each year—Sunday, Christmas, Easter, and so forth—set aside for worship and religious celebration.

Native American faiths, in contrast, either influenced or were affected by nearly every aspect of everyday life, including seemingly the most trivial ones. Osage scholar George E. Tinker explains it this way:

> The social structures and cultural traditions of American Indian peoples are infused with a spirituality that cannot be separated from, say, picking corn or tanning hides, hunting game or making war. Nearly every human act was accompanied by attention to religious details, sometimes out of practiced habit

For the Sioux tribes of the Midwest, the Black Hills in South Dakota carry great spiritual significance.

and sometimes with more specific ceremony. In the [American] Northwest, harvesting cedar bark would be accompanied by prayer and ceremony, just as killing a buffalo required ceremonial actions and words.... Among the Osages [of the American Midwest] the spiritual principle of respect for life dictated that the decision to go to war against another people usually required an eleven-day ceremony.[7]

Tinker's point that spirituality pervaded "nearly every human act" is well illustrated by some of the smaller customs of his own ancestors. Before and during the colonial era, the Osage divided each of their towns into two "grand divisions," one representing the religious concept of the sky, the other of the earth. It was thought that these divisions had to be in balance for life to continue and thrive. And to maintain this balance, people structured their lives accordingly. It was customary for someone from one grand division of a town to marry a person from the other division, for example. Moreover, people from one grand division slept on their right side

Common Themes in Indian Religion

According to University of Delaware historian Christine Leigh Heyrman, there are some general similarities among many of the Native American faiths. She writes:

First, at the time of European contact, all but the simplest indigenous cultures in North America had developed coherent religious systems that included cosmologies —creation myths, transmitted orally from one generation to the next, which purported to explain how those societies had come into being. Second, most native peoples worshiped an all-powerful, all-knowing Creator or "Master Spirit" (a being that assumed a variety of forms and both genders). They also venerated . . . a host of lesser supernatural entities, including an evil god who dealt out disaster, suffering, and death. Third and finally, the members of most tribes believed in the immortality of the human soul and an afterlife, the main feature of which was the abundance of every good thing that made earthly life secure and pleasant. Like all other cultures, the Indian societies of North America hoped to enlist the aid of the supernatural in controlling the natural and social world, and each tribe had its own set of religious observances devoted to that aim.

Christine Leigh Heyrman, "Native American Religion in Early America," National Humanities Center. http://nationalhumanitiescenter.org/tserve/eighteen/ekeyinfo/natrel.htm.

and put on their right shoe first each morning, while people on the other side of town slept on their left side and donned their left shoe first.

Most Native American faiths also had a strong spatial dimension, that is, the concept that spaces, or individual geographical places, had spiritual qualities. Most Christians have a more portable concept of religion. In other words, the spatial dimension of their faith is mainly in their minds and hearts, and they carry it with them wherever they go. One notable exception is their reverence for the Holy Land, in Palestine, where Jesus once lived and preached. Various spots in that region are seen as having spiritual significance.

Native American spatial spirituality was similar to the Christian reverence for the Holy Land, only even more ingrained in local peoples and their traditions. For the Sioux tribes of the Midwest, for instance, the Black Hills, in South Dakota, were sacred. And for the Iroquois of New York, Tawasentha, on the Hudson River, home of their cultural hero Hiawatha, had deep spiritual significance. When Indian peoples were forced to abandon such traditional sacred places, they felt they had lost a portion of their spirituality.

Part of this feeling that certain places were sacred stemmed from the common Native American belief that most or all aspects of nature are alive and, like people, endowed with spiritual power. This included what whites normally viewed as inanimate objects, such as mountains, trees, and rivers. This belief was one reason that Indian peoples tended to be good stewards of the land and largely refrained from reshaping and polluting it, as white settlers and developers repeatedly did. Tinker points out:

> The sense of the interrelationship of all creation—of all two-legged, four-legged, winged, and other living, moving things (from fish and rivers to rocks, trees, and mountains)—may be the most important contribution Indian peoples have made to the science and spirituality of the modern world.[8]

Souls and the Afterlife

Most other Native American religious beliefs varied widely from place to place, people to people, and tribe to tribe. A clear example of this diversity is seen in how they viewed the afterlife. On the one hand, most Indians held that human beings possess some sort of spirit, or soul, that lives on after death. But on the other hand, nearly every Native American group had its own, and at times quite distinctive, concept of what happens to the soul of a deceased person.

Some groups believed that a person's soul rose up into the sky and became a new star. In contrast, others thought that the opposite happened—that a dead person's spirit went to a subterranean (underground) realm similar to the underworld of the Greeks and Romans. Still other groups, including some Sioux tribes, envisioned that each person had four separate souls. The first, called the

Some Native American groups believed that a person's soul rose up into the sky and became a new star.

"spirit of the body," expired along with the body; the second soul lived on, but always stayed near the person's remains; the third lived on and traveled to a better place far to the east or south; and the fourth was a roving spirit that could, under certain circumstances, bring death and disease to living people.

One of the most unusual and interesting American Indian concepts of the afterlife is that of the Hidasta, a people of the northern plains. A diligent nineteenth-century scholar, Washington Matthews, studied Hidasta culture and made this observation about how its people envisioned the soul and afterlife:

When a Hidasta dies, his shade (soul) lingers four nights around the camp or village in which he died, and then goes to the lodge of his departed kindred [relatives] in the village of the dead. When he arrives there, he is rewarded for his valor, self-denial, and ambition on Earth by receiving the same regard in the one place as in the other; for there, as here, the brave man is honored the coward despised.[9]

Less noble and more materialistic was the way in which the Natchez Indians, who dwelled in what are now Louisiana and Alabama, conceived the afterlife. They believed that if one of their warriors followed society's rules, he would be rewarded with what a famous old adage calls "wine, women, and song." According to a Jesuit priest who visited the Natchez in 1699:

> The rewards of the afterlife to which they look forward consist principally in feasting [and] they think that those who have been the faithful observers of their laws will be conducted into a region of pleasures, where all kinds of exquisite [foodstuffs] will be furnished them in abundance, that their delightful and tranquil days will flow on in the midst of festivals, dances, and women. In short, they will revel in all imaginable pleasures.

Those who had broken society's laws, however, could expect to have a miserable existence in the great beyond:

> [They] will be cast upon lands unfruitful and entirely covered with water, where they will not have any kind of corn, but will be exposed entirely naked to the sharp bites of mosquitoes, that all nations will make war upon them, that they will never eat meat, and have no nourishment but the flesh of crocodiles, spoiled fish, and shell-fish.[10]

Creation Stories

Native American tales of creation and human origins also varied significantly from place to place and group to group. Practically every people and tribe had its own creation myths, although some familiar general themes ran through most of these stories. One modern researcher writes:

> A few tribes recognize a creator [who] generates the world and its inhabitants, but the usual conception is either of a pre-existent sky-world [or] else of a kind of cosmic womb from which the first people had their origin. . . . The next act of the world drama details the deeds of a hero or of twin heroes who are the shapers and lawgivers of the habitable earth. They conquer the primitive monsters [and] generally one of them is slain and passes to the underworld to become its lord.[11]

An example of the sky world appears in the creation story of the Cherokee, who lived in what is now Georgia and South Carolina. They held that earth was originally an island hanging on cords from the sky. It was dark at first until the creator

One creation theory of Native Americans involves the Sky Woman, who fell from the heavens and landed on an island that became North America.

On the Great Turtle's Back

The following passage comes from the version of the Iroquois creation myth set down by John Norton, a Mohawk who played a prominent role in the War of 1812.

In the beginning, before the formation of the Earth, the country above the sky was inhabited by Superior Beings, over whom the Great Spirit presided. His daughter having become pregnant . . . he pulled up a great tree by the roots and threw her through the cavity thereby formed, but to prevent her utter destruction he previously ordered the Great Turtle to get from the bottom of the waters [that then covered the universe] some slime on its back. . . . When she had fallen on the back of the Turtle, with the mud she found there she began to form the Earth, and by the time of her delivery had increased it to the extent of a little island. Her child was a daughter and as she grew up the Earth extended [even further] under their hands.

Quoted in Colin G. Calloway, ed., *The World Turned Upside Down: Indian Voices from Early America*. Boston: Bedford, 1994, p. 23.

allowed the sun to shine, after which he placed animals, plants, and people on earth. In Iroquois myths the sky is a divine character called the Sky Woman, who fell from the heavens onto an island made by a huge turtle. The island expanded into North America, and then the Sky Woman had a daughter, who gave birth to the first people.

Among the many mythical Indian heroes who killed monsters and paved the way for civilized societies, one of the most famous and fascinating is the sacred figure Lone Man, celebrated by the Mandan, who lived in what is now North Dakota. As the story begins, earth's surface is covered with water and no people yet exist. However, Lone Man does exist and one day, while walking on the surface of the water, he encounters a being named First Man. Each asks where the other had come from, but neither can remember; as far as they know, they had always been there.

Lone Man and First Man decide to make the world more livable. So they construct land, including mountains, valleys, and plains, from clods of dirt from the sea bottom. Then they create deer, cattle, sheep, buffalo, and other animals, which spread across the earth. A few years later, the two heroes come upon some humans—the Mandan—who are doing their best to survive by hunting, fishing, and growing corn. Neither Lone Man nor First Man has any idea where these people came from.

In time First Man says farewell and departs toward the west. But Lone Man remains with the Mandan, who continue to struggle just to get enough to eat. Taking pity on them, Lone Man decides he could help them more easily if he became human himself. After undergoing this miraculous conversion, he shows them how to fashion warmer clothes and find more food. He also saves them from destruction by defeating an evil monster named Maninga, which had taken the form of a great flood. Finally Lone Man says good-bye to the Mandan and, like First Man before him, departs toward the sunset.

Attempts to Convert Indians

Modern scholars point out some striking similarities between elements of the Lone Man creation story and several elements of the Christian Bible. In both, at first there is only water and it is dark. Then the creator brings forth both light and land. Later, a special being who has no beginning or end takes human form in order to help the human race. Many other similarities existed between Christian religious traditions and those of various Native American groups.

However, instead of finding these shared ideas fascinating and respecting the Indian traditions, most whites dismissed or condemned Native American religions. Many European colonists felt it was their duty to show the natives the error of their ways and convert them to the Christian faith. In this endeavor, there were some scattered successes. In Massachusetts, the Puritans translated the Bible for local Indians and set up so-

called praying towns in which converted natives lived. By 1674 about thirty such towns existed, with a total population of close to two thousand. Similarly, Jesuit priests managed to convert thousands of Indians in New York and southern Canada in the mid-1600s.

A missionary preaches to a group of Native Americans, attempting to convert them to Christianity.

Why Trees Lose Their Leaves

The Cherokee, who originally lived in what is now Georgia, have a colorful creation story, excerpted below.

Long ago, before there were any people, the earth was a great island floating in a sea of water, suspended by four cords hanging down from the sky vault, which was made of solid rock. It was dark and the animals could not see, so they got the sun and set it in a track to go across the island every day from east to west, just overhead. The Creator told the animals and plants to stay awake for seven nights. But only a few of the animals were able to, including owls and panthers, and they were rewarded with the power to go about in the dark. Among the plants, only the cedars, pines, spruces, and laurels stayed awake, so they were allowed to remain green year-round and to provide the best medicines. The Creator chided the other trees: "Because you have not endured to the end, you shall lose your hair every winter." People appeared last, after the animals, the sun, and the plants, but they multiplied so quickly that they threatened to overrun the world. So it was decided that each woman would have only one child a year, and it has been that way ever since.

Quoted in James J. Cassidy Jr., ed., *Through Indian Eyes: The Untold Story of Native American Peoples.* Pleasantville, NY: Reader's Digest, 1995, p. 37.

According to the Cherokee, their creator made the cedar tree stay green year-round to provide the best medicines.

Short of complete conversion, some natives were at least influenced by Christian ideas. And on occasion, old Indian beliefs and Christian beliefs merged in what was essentially a new religion. The most notable example was in the Carolinas, where between 1700 and 1740, with native populations dwindling, more than a dozen Indian groups came together to form a new Indian nation— the Catawba. The new society had its own religion, which borrowed elements from both Native American faiths and Christianity.

Overall, however, most Indians neither converted to Christianity nor adopted any Christian beliefs during the colonial period. Moreover, whites annihilated many tribes or severely brutalized and/or exiled others, in the process doing irreparable harm to or even destroying many native belief systems. And throughout this process, whites were highly intolerant of the native beliefs.

In retrospect it is ironic that the white Christians of that era were often intolerant toward each other, a kind of hypocrisy that was not lost on many Indians. While trying to convert some New York natives, a Boston missionary told them that their own religions were false and that there was only one proper way to worship the "Great Spirit." One local Indian leader responded in part, "You say there is but one way to worship and serve the Great Spirit. If there is but one religion, why do you white people differ so much about it?"[12] Saying that the colonists "differed" about religion was actually an understatement. Colonial America had become quite literally the most religiously diverse, as well as religiously competitive, place on earth.

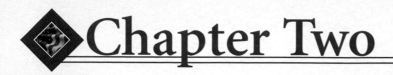

Chapter Two

A GREAT DIVERSITY OF FAITHS

There is no doubt that large numbers of modern Americans are religiously devout. A recent major poll found that six in ten American adults feel that religious faith is very important in their lives. Only 15 percent said they have no religion at all. Yet as heavily weighted in favor of religion as these figures are, they reflect a level of religious devoutness considerably lower than that of colonial times. Simply put, in those days religious beliefs and activities played a much larger role in people's everyday lives. Louis B. Wright, a noted scholar of colonial times, points out that when a modern person

> tries to project himself into the period of his colonial ancestors, one of his greatest difficulties is a comprehension of the pervasiveness of religion and its universal influence upon

men, women, and children of the earlier age. . . . Whatever [people] believed, they believed with greater devotion than most of their descendants display today. That is not to say that our ancestors were more virtuous than we, but that they were more God-fearing. When the wicked sinned, more of them trembled in fear of eternal damnation.[13]

Yet people's level of devotion to God was only one part of the picture of colonial religion. An even bigger part was the sheer diversity of the religious beliefs that grew and spread in the English North American colonies. Today many people assume that most colonists had more or less the same beliefs. Another common assumption is that they were all Christians. And still another is that most colonists were either Puritans or were at least puritanical, or very strict and narrow, in their beliefs. These suppositions are all mistaken. The truth is that the earliest settlers represented several different religious groups. And as time went on, some of the colonies came to feature an almost bewildering variety of belief systems, including both Christian and non-Christian ones.

Hoping to Build a Heavenly City

Only in the first few decades of colonization and in a few specific places was there a lack of religious diversity. Whatever truth exists in the stereotype of narrow-minded settlers who were intolerant of people of other faiths was exemplified most by the Puritans in Massachusetts. They differed from separatist groups like the Pilgrims (founders of Plymouth Colony), who wanted a complete break with the Church of England, or Anglican Church. The early Puritans desired to remain Anglican but sought to reform the church. It needed to be purified, they felt, by simplifying a number of rituals and eliminating bishops and other high church officials, among other things.

Once the Puritans established a firm base in Massachusetts Bay Colony, however, they broke with the Anglicans and became what are often called Congregationalists. (In general, Congregationalists are groups in which members of the congregation, rather than distant religious officials, run a local church.) The early Puritans were suspicious not only

of other faiths, but also of democracy. They wanted a society in which a few respected local religious leaders controlled the populace and made sure everyone was God-fearing and righteous. Their ideal was stated concisely and famously by Puritan leader John Winthrop. In 1630, in a sermon titled "A Model of Christian Charity," he stated in part:

[We must] rejoice together, mourn together, labor, and suffer together, always having before our eyes our commission and community in the work. . . . The Lord will be our God and delight to dwell among us, as his own people and will command a blessing upon us in all our ways. . . . For we must consider that we shall be as a city upon a hill, the eyes of all people are upon us; so that if we shall deal falsely with our God in this work we have undertaken and so cause him to withdraw his present help from us, we shall be made a [shameful] story and a byword through the world. . . . Therefore let us choose life, that we, and our seed, may live by obeying his voice.[14]

To ensure that everyone in society adhered to these lofty principles, Puritan leaders made and enforced strict laws. Anyone who disagreed with those leaders on spiritual matters was branded a criminal. And a person who failed to attend church was whipped. Meanwhile, almost all forms of play and recreation were banned. In addition, Puritan

A drummer calls colonists to worship in the 1600s. In the first few decades of settlement, there was not much religious diversity.

religious services were extremely lengthy. According to noted scholar Jon Butler, a typical service, "consisted of an opening prayer, a reading from the Bible, psalm singing, a sermon, another singing of a psalm, a prayer, and a concluding blessing. The entire service might last three to four hours. . . . The concluding prayer [itself] often lasted an hour."[15]

Over time, however, religious worship in the Massachusetts colony, and elsewhere in America, became less strict. Much of this was the result of economic developments, especially increasing prosperity. Historian John C. Miller writes:

Among the enemies of the life dedicated to the glorification of God and the erection of a Heavenly City upon earth, the chief was economic prosperity. In America, the churches of the poor and downtrodden became middle-class churches, and in the process they lost much of their original fervor and mystical idealism. The only thing that the otherworldly sects could not endure was economic success. They thrived upon persecution and poverty but their sense of dedication was undermined by the sense of having arrived economically and socially. Unknowingly, [the stricter] religious [groups] contained within themselves the seeds of their own destruction. The Puritan doctrine

that success in one's calling was [evidence] of divine favor became, with the passage of time, a justification for pursuing worldly ends.[16]

Massachusetts and other areas of New England became not only less strict about daily behavior but also more open to other ideas. Through ordinary commerce, for example, some Puritans got to know people of other denominations, including Anglicans. In 1687 the first traditional Anglican services were held in Massachusetts Bay Colony. That same year work began on King's Chapel, the first Anglican church in Boston. And soon afterward the English crown issued the colony a new charter that made it unlawful to exclude

Puritan Ideas Linger On

Although the Puritans themselves are gone, the rich heritage of their religious and social ideas still affects modern America. Noted scholar Louis B. Wright writes:

The stern and grim religion of the Puritans, so alien to the spirit of the modern world, bequeathed [handed down] social doctrines that have had their influence upon later American history. [Americans] have not yet entirely abandoned the notion of the value of work as an end in itself. The belief that idleness is sin is deep-seated in the American char-

acter and helps to explain a persistent application to duty that has brought material success to many Americans. The Puritans were also convinced that they were the elect of God, the chosen people, and that doctrine, too, has helped to shape American character. Americans in general have found it easy to believe that we enjoy the especial favor of the Almighty and that our ways should be adopted by all other people. Perhaps that is a direct heritage from the Puritans.

Louis B. Wright, *Everyday Life in Colonial America.* New York: Putnam's, 1965, p. 180.

Anglicans from local worship. The Puritan stranglehold on religious expression had been broken, and similar trends toward diversity continued in the decades that followed.

An Explosion of Diversity

Meanwhile, in most of the colonies lying south of New England, religious diversity had come earlier. One reason for this was that a few outspoken and courageous individuals among the early settlers broke away from stricter groups like the Puritans and set up their own more tolerant and diverse colonies. A prominent example is Roger Williams. He repeatedly questioned the policies and authority of the leaders of Massachusetts Bay Colony; so in 1635 they banished him. He ended up establishing Rhode Island, which was much more welcoming of other faiths. Similarly, William Penn joined the Quakers, who had also broken away from the Puritans, and founded Pennsylvania. From the start, that colony was a haven for a wide range of Christian groups, of which the Quakers were only one.

Another reason that several of the mid-Atlantic colonies developed religious diversity early on was that most of these colonies were quite large, making compact religious organization and enforcement, like that in Massachusetts, very difficult. According to scholar Edward G. Gray:

in these sprawling colonies [people] were simply too widely scattered for

officials to be able to keep track of their religious activities. And the resources of the established church were simply inadequate to provide churches and ministers to service such far-flung populations. The collective result was that . . . colonial government lacked the capacity to compel colonists to adhere to any single religious persuasion or denomination.[17]

Several non-Puritan settlers moved south of New England, hoping to establish more diverse colonies. The founder of Pennsylvania, William Penn, was one of them. He became a Quaker.

Interfaith Marriages

Because of the widespread religious diversity and toleration in the colonies, it was not unusual for people of differing faiths to fall in love and get married. That did not mean, however, that all the relatives always approved. In the following excerpt from a surviving letter, a Jewish woman expresses her distress at learning that her daughter has secretly married an Anglican man.

Good God, what a shock it was when they [told] me she had left the house and had been married six months. I can hardly hold my pen while I am writing it. . . . I had heard the report of her [want-

ing] to be married to [the wealthy Anglican] Oliver DeLancey, but [did not believe it, so I] gave no heed to it. . . . I shall never have that serenity nor peace within [that] I have so happily had hitherto [in the past]. My house has been my prison ever since. I had not heart enough to go near the street door. It's a pain to me to think about going again to town, and if [my husband's] business would permit him to live out[side] of it, I never would go near it again.

Quoted in Leo Hershkowitz and Isidor S. Meyer, eds., *Letters of the Franks Family (1733–1748)*. Waltham, MA: American Jewish Historical Society, 1968, pp. 116–19.

Particularly expansive religious diversity developed in New York, which began as the Dutch colony of New Netherland but was seized by the English in 1664. In 1683 a Catholic named Thomas Dongan arrived from England to take charge as the colony's new governor. And he was astounded by the variety of beliefs and denominations he found there. The Dutch Reformed Church was still thriving, as were a number of Quaker groups. There were also Catholics, French Calvinists, Anglicans, Baptists (Christians similar to Congregationalists but who advocated baptizing adults instead of infants), Jews, and other groups. Moreover, the members of the largest group had no organized religion at all. Dongan summed it up this way: "Of all sort of opinion there are some, and the most part [are] of none at all."[18]

The New York religious melting pot is only one example of spiritual diversity in the colonies between 1690 and 1770. In South Carolina most of the early settlers were Anglicans. But by the end of 1770, the colony featured many Scotch Presbyterians. (Early Presbyterians were similar to Congregationalists and Baptists except that they baptized infants and had overriding church governments called "presbyteries" or "synods.") South Carolina also witnessed large influxes of Quakers and German Lutherans. Similarly, Maryland began as a Catholic refuge but also welcomed other groups. And the colony's Catholics were quickly outnumbered by Anglicans and other Protestants. Georgia became even more religiously diverse, eventually featuring a healthy mix of Anglicans, Catholics, Lutherans, Congregationalists, Presbyterians, Baptists, and others. Finally toward the end of the colonial period, Methodists, reformed Anglicans who stressed human free will and various methods of obtaining God's grace, began to spread through several of the colonies.

By the mid-1700s, the veritable explosion of religious diversity had caused many colonists to become disoriented and in some cases even turned off by religion. According to one observer writing in North Carolina in the 1760s, people often complained to him that they were "being eaten up by itinerant teachers, preachers and imposters." The observer also writes, "By the variety of tailors who would pretend to know [how] Christ's coat is to be worn, none will put it on. And among the various plans of religion, they are at loss which to adapt, and consequently are without any religion at all."[19]

The Great Awakening

The observer's mention of "itinerant teachers, preachers and imposters" was mainly a reference to a large-scale religious movement that became known as the great awakening. It swept through the colonies, lasting from about 1734 to 1744. Partly because of widespread economic prosperity, church attendance had fallen off in some regions in the years immediately preceding the awakening. And a new brand of fiery preachers sought to revive religious fervor. The most famous and influential among them were Jonathan Edwards, a Massachusetts minister, and George Whitefield, a follower of John Wesley, founder of the Methodists. Edwards tried to whip worshippers into a frenzy by instilling in them fear of hell and damnation. Whitefield called on sinners to repent their sins. And his oratory was so effective that many fell on the floor before him, weeping and begging for forgiveness.

One contemporary observer, Charles Chauncy, a more traditional minister, witnessed several such displays, which he saw as revolting and harmful to both religion and society. He did not like that these evangelic preachers seemed to have a particularly strong influence on teenage girls and children. And he was appalled by the sight of wild outbursts of extreme religious fervor, often in church. In a 1742 letter to a friend, he called such behavior "a scandal to all who call themselves Christians," then added:

> There is the screaming and shrieking to the greatest degree; and the persons thus affected are generally children, young people, and women.... These meetings they would continue till ten, eleven, twelve o'clock at night; in the midst of them, sometimes ten, twenty, thirty, and sometimes many

more would scream and cry out, or send forth the most lamentable groans, while others made exertions of joy by clapping their hands, uttering ecstatic [overjoyed] expressions, singing psalms, [and] some would swoon [faint] away under the influence of distressing fears and others swallowed up with insupportable joy. While some were fainting, others labored under convulsive twitches of body. . . . For myself, I am among those who are clearly in the opinion that there never was such a spirit of superstition and enthusiasm reigning in the land before; never such gross disorders and barefaced affronts to common decency.[20]

The emotional gatherings and zealous sermons of the great awakening helped to swell the ranks of the Baptists and Methodists, who were not bothered by such emotional outbursts in church. But they steadily discredited the movement among average, more traditional worshippers, who saw such behavior as undignified. And that brought about the awakening's swift decline. No single preacher contributed more to this decline than the controversial James Davenport. A witness to one of his sermons, given in March 1743 in Connecticut, later recalled how Davenport inflamed the crowd so much that people ran to the town square and began burning the standard religious books of the day: "While the books were in flames, they cried out: 'Thus the souls of the authors

During the great awakening, Massachusetts minister Jonathan Edwards instilled fear of hell and damnation among worshippers with his sermons.

of those books . . . are roasting in the flames of hell.'" The next day Davenport accused his listeners of "idolizing their own apparel" and got them to strip off their clothes. The clothes "must be burned,"[21] he said, and proceeded to take off his own pants and toss them into the flames.

Such extreme conduct was too much for most colonists. According to Wright, "many conventional folk, disgusted with the unrestrained excesses of the evangelists, went over to the Anglican communion, where respectable people might worship with decorum, untroubled by a noisy preacher shouting that they were damned."[22] The great awakening therefore faded from view by the mid-1740s. Nevertheless, it had permanently altered the American religious landscape by increasing the number of devout Christian worshippers.

Non-Christian Groups

Christians were not the only pious people in the colonies, however. In addition to the many and varied Native American groups, each with its own distinctive faith, there were also Jews and African servants and slaves. Like many Christians, the Jews who crossed the Atlantic to North America did so seeking religious freedom. Jews had long been widely persecuted across Europe and even expelled from some countries, notably Spain.

The first Jews in the colonies arrived in New Netherland in 1654. More came in the years that followed, and in 1695 the first permanent synagogue in British America was erected in New York City. By the 1720s, 2 percent of that city's population was Jewish. And Jews also settled in Charleston, South Carolina; Philadelphia, Pennsylvania; and Newport, Rhode Island, among other urban areas. Although they achieved religious freedom, they could not escape intolerance and persecution; many were prohibited from voting and some were verbally abused and physically attacked.

Like most settlers, Jews came to North America seeking religious freedom. The first synagogue in British America, Congregation Shearith Israel, was erected in the late 1600s in New York City.

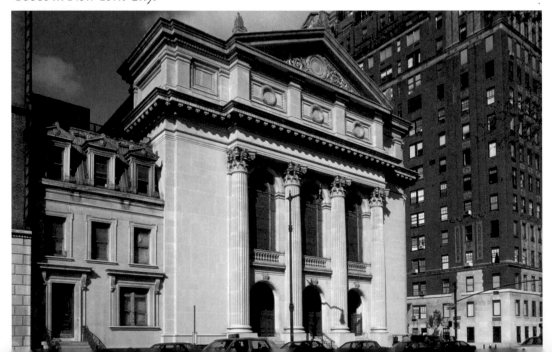

Prison Time for Swearing

According to Quaker law, anyone who used God's name while swearing had to pay a fine or be imprisoned for five days.

Although they were more liberal than the Puritans, the Quakers were considerably less religiously tolerant in colonial times than they are today, as evidenced by several laws they passed in Pennsylvania in the late 1600s. For example, only those who "profess and declare they believe in Jesus Christ to be the son of God" could vote or hold public office. And saying anything that defamed Jesus or using his or God's name while swearing was punished harshly. One law stated, "Whosoever shall swear in their common conversation by the name of God or Christ or Jesus, being legally convicted thereof, shall pay, for every such offense, five shillings, or suffer five days imprisonment in the house of correction at hard labor [and] be fed with bread and water only during that time."

Quoted in W. Keith Kavenagh, ed., *Foundations of Colonial America: A Documentary History*, vol. 2. New York: Chelsea House, 1983, pp. 1340–41.

This engraving depicts colonial Virginians after church service in the 1700s. Anglicans were well established in Virginia.

As for the Africans forcibly brought to North America, many held on to their ancestral religious beliefs as long as they could. Some thoughtful European observers noted that several African faiths had a supreme deity not unlike the Christian one. One difference was that the African deity was said to have created a number of lesser gods. Also, many African worshippers did not pray to their chief god because they saw him as too lofty to care about humans. Also common in many African faiths were divination (predicting the future by observing natural occurrences such as animal behavior) and communicating with deceased ancestors.

Little written documentation of these African faiths has survived. One exception is a tract penned by Olaudah

Equiano, a colonial slave who gained his freedom and became highly educated. He writes that the Ibo, a West-African people,

> believe that there is one Creator of all things, and that he lives in the sun. [They] believe he governs events, especially our deaths or captivity, but as for the doctrine of eternity, I do not remember to ever have heard of it. Some, however, believe in [reincarnation] in a certain degree. . . . Though we had no places of public worship, we had priests and magicians, or wise men. [They] calculated our time, and foretold [future] events.[23]

Jewish, African, and other non-Christian beliefs were in a sense extra spices in an already rich melting pot of colonial faiths. One thing that made the American religious scene remarkable in the 1700s, as one expert observer says, was that it did not consist of "a single story." It was instead a "convergence of a whole host of different stories . . . all engaged in the common struggle to satisfy their spiritual needs."[24]

Chapter Three

CLERGYMEN, WORSHIPPERS, AND CHURCHES

The wide diversity of religious beliefs that developed in British America in the late 1600s and early 1700s profoundly affected the lives of individuals and families, as well as society as a whole. This can be seen in even a brief examination of the three principal aspects of the religious scene in that era. These are the members of the clergy, the churchgoers who made up their flocks, and the churches themselves.

The experiences of ministers and other clergymen who arrived in the colonies around 1700 or so are good examples. These eager, intrepid individuals "entered a strange and disorienting world," notes New York University scholar Patricia U. Bonomi. She continues:

Confronting them everywhere but in New England was a scene of scattered congregations, competing sects, a chronic shortage of fellow clergymen, and few of the supports that undergirdled [supported] ministerial authority in the Old World. There were no bishops . . . to ordain and discipline ministers for the Anglican, Lutheran, and [most other] churches. Theological education did not exist outside of New England. [Also] salaries [for clergymen were small and] uncertain, and tenure [guaranteed job security] insecure. . . . Some clergymen found this alien environment so unsettling that they returned home at the first opportunity.[25]

But many of these men did stay and make an earnest attempt to help new groups of colonists organize congregations; they also ensured that existing groups of parishioners could continue to practice their faiths. Over time this allowed each of the many and varied denominations in the colonies to grow and prosper. That was good not only for these individual faiths, but also for the people within them. Upholding religious diversity allowed them to choose the approach to worship that best suited their individual spiritual needs.

It was also good for society as a whole because the idea of religious freedom and diversity became strongly ingrained in the fabric of colonial life. And that laid the groundwork for guarantees of religious freedom later included in the Constitution by the U.S. founding fathers. Meanwhile, as individual faiths and congregations grew and thrived, they could afford to build bigger and more splendid churches; these became symbols of economic prosperity and community pride as well as the piety of the parishioners.

Trying to Gain Trust and Influence

Reaching the high degree of organization and influence American churches possessed on the eve of the American Revolution was a long and difficult struggle. Most of the early colonists were rugged individualists. And when it came to religion, more often than not they wanted to be independent of the authority of the religious groups and leaders in England and other parts of Europe. That made them very wary of new ministers and other clergymen who came from those places. So such new arrivals often had

trouble adjusting and establishing relationships of trust between themselves and their flocks. Yet the need for these ministers from the far side of the ocean was great. Especially in the colonies south of New England, there was a serious shortage of trained clergymen in the first half of the colonial era.

The difficulties experienced by the developing Anglican groups in the colonies provide a clear example of the problems faced by nearly all the early denominations. Anglicans in England desired to see their faith, which already had a foothold in Virginia, Maryland, and several other colonies, continue to spread and prosper. To further this goal, in 1701 they established the Society for the Propagation of the Gospel in Foreign Parts. Its chief function was to ensure a steady supply of new, trained ministers for the colonies.

Even in Virginia, where the Anglican Church was well established, however, the early ministers encountered resistance and sometimes even hostility. First, the Virginians opposed having a bishop, even one stationed in London, to make and enforce local church rules. Instead, members of local vestries insisted that they make the rules, as well as hire and fire ministers as they saw fit. (A vestry was a committee of locals, almost always men, who were elected to administer their church's affairs.)

It took a long time, therefore, for local vestries and churchgoers to learn to completely trust and delegate major authority to individual ministers. Instrumental in this process in Virginia was Scottish-born James Blair. Ambitious and dedicated to strengthening church authority, he became Virginia's leading Anglican minister in 1690 and remained so for fifty-three years. Little by little during that period, he earned the trust of local vestries and worshippers. And in time he managed to raise the status of Virginia's Anglican ministers, who became more professional, independent, influential, and most important of all, trusted by the people.

Some opponents of a more organized and powerful local clergy continued to resist such efforts. Often they accused ministers of being corrupt, lazy, and drunkards. And undoubtedly some were. However, modern studies suggest that no more than 10 percent of Virginia's Anglican clergymen fell into this unfortunate category. The truth of the situation was summed up by a Virginian named Hugh Jones in 1724. Most local ministers, he said, "have a mind to do their duty [and] may live with as much satisfaction, respect, comfort, and love as most clergymen in England."[26]

Many early clergymen encountered difficulties in other colonies as well. In Maryland, for example, governors sometimes chose ministers themselves and imposed them on parishes and vestries, which led to clashes with local parishioners. Worshippers in one local parish locked an unwanted minister out of the church. In desperation, he climbed through a window and tried to reach the pulpit, but the angry people showered him with small stones, at which point he pulled out a pistol and threatened to shoot them.

From Hard Times to Fiery Sermons

Even in situations in which ministers of various denominations were accepted and respected, they often faced various logistical troubles and hardships. Particularly in the larger colonies, such as Pennsylvania, Virginia, and the Carolinas, individual parishes were very large. One South Carolina parish measured 80 by 130 miles (129km by 209km)—a total of more than 10,000 square miles (25,900 sq. km). In comparison, parishes in the mother country averaged 5 square miles (13 sq. km).

To preach to and look after the needs of worshippers scattered across such large parishes, many ministers were forced to become itinerant, or traveling, clergymen. It was common, for instance, for a minister to hold services or perform marriages or baptisms, in people's homes or barns, in five, six, or more widely spaced locations in a single week. This necessitated hundreds of miles of travel by horse or wagon, usually over rough dirt roads. Quite often there were no roads at all. One Pennsylvania minister complained about having to travel 1,632 miles (2,626km) in one year. And in Virginia a preacher complained that his health was ruined by his itinerant lifestyle, in which he often traveled 50 miles (80km) at a stretch through swamps

Because worshippers were spread across large parishes, ministers often had to travel great distances to perform services. Weddings were often officiated in people's homes.

and across rivers. He was, he said, "much impaired by being exposed to the excess of the weather," which was "very hot in the summer and piercing cold in the winter, and always variable."[27]

Other problems faced by clergymen were like those that plagued William Harrison, an Anglican minister who began preaching in New Jersey in 1722. Most members of his flock were too poor to contribute to his salary, which as a result remained very low. Also, it was common for many worshippers to skip church on Sunday because they lived so far away. In addition, when Harrison traveled to people's homes, he found them depressingly small and squalid, and many of the foods

they offered him were distasteful. He begged his superiors in the Society for the Propagation of the Gospel to allow him to return to England. But instead they reassigned him to Staten Island, off the coast of New York. There he conducted services in a small church that remained unfinished for many years, and he had to become a part-time farmer to help make ends meet.

Meanwhile, most ministers in New England had it far easier. First, the Congregationalists had no shortage of trained clergy, in part because of Harvard College and other schools that educated ministers. Harvard alone turned out 987 ministers between 1691 and 1760.

Also, congregations and parishes were small in the region, so there was little need for itinerant clergymen.

But like ministers throughout the colonies, those in New England did have to cater to the needs of the worshippers and to changing trends in the manner in which church services were performed. For example, over time it became clear that sermons lasting two or more hours, which were common in the 1600s, were too long for many worshippers. By the 1730s, therefore, most sermons lasted an hour or less.

Whatever their length, sermons remained the chief form of public expression for the clergy and their principal tool for connecting with and inspiring their flocks. Many ministers therefore put much time and effort into crafting

Sermons were the primary mode of communication and expression for the clergy, so they often lasted two hours or more.

Beware of Phony Preachers

In many colonial parishes, especially in areas settled by German groups who had few or no qualified ministers, charlatans were common. New York University scholar Patricia U. Bonomi explains:

So eager were the provincials [country folk] to hear sermons and to partake of church sacraments that any self-proclaimed preacher who came within range might be called into service. With no Lutheran or Reformed synods [church councils] to authenticate ordination papers . . . false claims and forged documents were a commonplace. [Thus] a number of noto-rious charlatans wandered through the colonies preaching sermons patched to-gether out of books and offering com-munion "for cash in hand." One such mountebank [phony trickster], touting himself as the Prince of Württemburg turned Lutheran preacher, was driven out of Georgia, only to turn up in Penn-sylvania, where he was reported roving [around] "whoring, stealing, gluttonizing [overeating], and swilling [getting drunk]."

Patricia U. Bonomi, *Under the Cope of Heaven: Religion, Society, and Politics in Colonial America.* New York: Ox-ford University Press, 2003, p. 77.

these speeches to achieve maximum ef-fect. According to Bonomi:

Ministers of the early eighteenth century shaped sermons to appeal both to the minds and hearts of their flock. The message was in-tended to be readily understood and to accord with experience and reason. Frequently sermons were directed toward specific [persons] in the congregation, such as women, youths, or servants. . . . Preaching was expected to be learned but not os-tentatious [showy], neither flowery nor [overly loud], but warm enough to stir emotions.[28]

In contrast, much louder and more fiery sermons became the rage among the leading preachers of the great awak-ening. And these speeches, which were frequently more like performances, often made major and lasting impressions on those who witnessed them. A Connecti-cut carpenter named Nathan Cole at-tended a lecture by George Whitefield in 1739 and later recalled:

When I saw Mr. Whitefield come upon the scaffold, he looked almost angelical. [He was] a young, slim, slender youth before some thousands of people with a bold undaunted countenance [manner], [and] he

Spiritually Revived by a Preacher

The speeches of many of the ministers of the great awakening deeply moved listeners, especially people who had come to have doubts about their faith. A Rhode Island woman, Sarah Osborne, left behind a fond remembrance of hearing one of these ministers, Gilbert Tennent, preach:

When Mr. Tennent came soon after, it pleased God to bless his preaching so to me that it roused me. But I was all the winter after exercised with dreadful doubts and fears about my [spiritual] state. I questioned the truth of all I had experienced. . . . Then it pleased God to return Mr. Tennent to us again, and he preached twenty-one sermons here. . . . [Before that] I had lost the sensible manifestations of Christ's love, [and Mr. Tennent] struck directly at those things. . . . After I was thus [spiritually] revived [by hearing his words], my longings to be made useful in the world returned, and I earnestly pleaded with God that he would not suffer me to live any longer an unprofitable servant, but would point out some way in which I might be useful.

Quoted in Nancy F. Cott et al., eds., *Root of Bitterness: Documents of the Social History of American Women*. Boston, MA: Northeastern University Press, 1996, p. 52.

looked as if he was clothed with the authority from the Great God [and] my hearing him preach gave me a heart wound [filled my heart with hope]. By God's blessing, my old foundation [way of viewing religious matters] was broken up, and I saw that my righteousness would not save me. . . . All that I could do would not save me, and he had decreed from eternity who should be saved and who not.[29]

Worshippers' Varied Needs

Composing sermons of the right length and content was only one way that clergymen met (or in some cases exploited) worshippers' needs. The most successful ministers understood that colonial Americans joined religious groups and attended church for a wide variety of reasons. Being pious and wanting to connect with and serve God was only the most obvious one.

Another motivation for religious worship, for example, was the strong need many felt for community. At the time churches were places not only for worshipping but also for conversing, sharing life experiences, and passing on news and gossip. In addition, belonging to a church met a number of family needs, including religious education of children and carrying on various family spiritual traditions.

The major connection between family life and churchgoing in the colonies affected the roles women played in both spheres. This is because women, though politically and often socially second-class citizens, were highly influential within the home. For this reason, over time colonial women took more responsibility for children's education, including moral guidance. And similarly, in the 1700s women assumed increasingly larger roles in religious matters than they had in the previous century. "Besides spiritual refreshment," one expert points out,

> religion offered women of energy and intellect an outlet to the wider world, as well as opportunities for self-expression, personal growth, and even leadership. Many women spoke with authority about complex theological issues. William Byrd II recorded that his wife and sister-in-law spent one evening [in] "fierce dispute about the infallibility of the Bible." [And] in New England, the religious writings of such pious matrons as Elizabeth Cotton and Jerusha Mather Oliver were incorporated into sermons or published for the enlightenment of a wider audience.[30]

From Plainness to Splendor

Devout women were also strong motivators in getting their children and husbands to attend church. Church attendance in the colonies was usually highest in New England, partly because it had a large number of established, well-maintained churches. In 1750, for instance, the city of Boston alone had eighteen churches to serve its population of fifteen thousand.

The earliest churches, in New England and in other parts of British America, were small, plain, and impermanent. The first church in Sudbury, Massachusetts, erected in 1643, for example, measured only 20 by 30 feet (6m by 9m) and had a thatch roof and a few rough wooden benches for seating. Even when larger towns like Boston, New York, and

Economic prosperity in the early 1700s allowed the colonists to build larger, more prominent churches, like the Old North Church in Boston.

The Magnificent Trinity Church

Although the earliest colonial churches were small and simple, over time new and in some cases magnificent ones were erected across the colonies. One of the finest and most famous was New York City's Trinity Church. A rebuilt version still exists today. The land for the first version of the Anglican structure was purchased in 1696 by the Church of England, and the parish received its charter the following year. The initial building went up in 1698. Its exact size and layout are somewhat uncertain, but when it was expanded in 1737 it measured 148 feet (45m) long and had a chancel (area containing the altar) 72 feet (22m) wide. That version of the church burned down in a terrible fire that ravaged the city in 1776, and it was not until 1790 that a new one was completed. A spire 281 feet (86m) high was added later and remained the highest point in New York City until 1890. In 1976 Trinity Church, once one of the foremost colonial houses of worship, was designated a National Historic Landmark.

The Trinity Church in New York was one of the most magnificent churches built in the 1700s, and became a National Historic Landmark in 1976.

Philadelphia began building larger, more permanent churches, those in most rural areas long remained small and simple; this was mainly because the tiny, scattered congregations in the countryside usually could not afford to erect and maintain large-scale buildings.

After 1680, and especially in the early 1700s, widespread economic prosperity in the colonies allowed parishioners in cities and even in many smaller towns to build many larger, more elaborate, and more permanent churches. Noted scholar Jon Butler writes:

> Colonial cities became centers of ecclesiastical [religious] splendor. Although New York City lacked a single church steeple in 1680, four pierced the skyline by 1720 and more were added in the next decades. In Philadelphia, Anglican, Presbyterian, Baptist, [and other]

churches constructed between 1720 and 1750 transformed the skyline of a city previously known only for its quiet Quaker meetinghouses.[31]

It should be noted that although many later colonial churches were large and beautifully decorated, they were not always comfortable. Very few had any sort of heating system. So in the depth of winter, churchgoers kept their coats on during the service. And it was not uncommon for the communion bread to freeze. This did little to discourage church attendance, however. Most colonial Americans were not only more devout and serious about religion than most modern Americans, but they were also hardier and more accustomed to physical discomforts. As in all historical times and places, a majority of people tended to accept grudgingly those things over which they had little or no control.

Chapter Four

FRINGE BELIEFS AND SUPERSTITIONS

When examining the belief systems current in British America in the 1600s and 1700s, the natural tendency is to focus on organized religious groups, such as Puritans, Quakers, Anglicans, Baptists, Catholics, and Jews. Often given little attention or ignored altogether are a wide array of alternative beliefs that, for the sake of convenience, can be collectively called fringe beliefs.

Fringe beliefs might also be called occult beliefs. Today experts tend to equate the occult with ideas or events related to the paranormal, the supernatural, magic, superstition, astrology, and/or mysticism. Included on the long list of beings and practices associated with these fringe areas are evil spirits, witches, demons, and ghosts; sorcery, necromancy (black magic), curses, and magical cures; speaking to or raising the dead; satanic pos-session and exorcisms; psychic powers and reincarnation; explaining human behavior through the movements of the stars and other heavenly bodies; and predicting the future, often through divination (studying animal behaviors and other natural occurrences).

Every being and practice on this list had at least some devout adherents in the American colonies. And several, including witches, demons, satanic possession, and astrology, were so widely accepted that they were considered common knowledge. Moreover, for many colonists, acceptance of such fringe beliefs often coexisted with their mainstream religious beliefs. In other words, one might accept the tenets of the Anglican Church and believe in witches and sorcery; similarly, a person who faithfully attended Catholic Mass every Sunday might also consult astrologers and diviners about planting crops and having children. Quite often the vast majority of avid believers in the major faiths just as strongly believed that witches, magic, and a long list of superstitions were real. According to scholar Edward G. Gray, millions of ordinary, devoutly religious colonists

regularly turned to the supernatural to help them understand their world. The popular belief in witchcraft is only the best-known expression of this. Other, more mundane examples abounded, [including]

the idea that the movement of celestial bodies—stars, moon, and planets—could help to predict weather, crop yields, and assorted other natural events.[32]

A Host of Superstitions

Believing that the stars and other heavenly bodies affect natural events on earth was only one of a host of superstitions, or unscientific folk beliefs, widely accepted in colonial America. This particular superstition did not overlap with established religious beliefs. But others

Of Stars and Facial Blemishes

Most colonists in British America who read almanacs and looked to astrology, the moon, stars, and planets for guidance in daily life were influenced by the writings of England's leading astrologer, William Lilly (1602–1681). His widely popular book Christian Astrology, *published in 1647, explains how nature and movements of the heavenly bodies affect human lives and societies. In the following excerpt, Lilly explains how the first of the so-called twelve houses of heaven might affect some people's faces.*

It has signification of the life of man, of the stature, color, complexion, form and shape of him. . . . It signifies the common people [and] as it is the first house, it represents the head and face of man, so that . . . at the time of birth, you shall observe . . . some blemish in the face, or in that member appropriate to the sign that then is upon the cusp of the house . . . the mark, mole, or scar is without fail in the head or face; and if few degrees of the sign ascend, the mark is in the upper part of the head; if the middle of the sign be on the cusp, the mole, mark or scar is in the middle of the face, or near it; if the later degrees ascend, the face is blemished near the chin, towards the neck. This I have found true in hundreds of examples.

William Lilly, *Christian Astrology Modestly Treated of in Three Books.* London: Brudenell, 1647. www.skyscript .co.uk/lilly_houses.html.

Practices such as witchery, sorcery, and satanic possession had followers in the American colonies.

52   Religious Beliefs in Colonial America

did. For example, certain specific kinds of natural events, especially large-scale disasters, were generally attributed to God's wrath. This included not only floods, earthquakes, and hurricanes, but also human wars and rebellions. When a large-scale Indian uprising caused the deaths of more than 350 settlers in Virginia in 1622, for instance, many of the surviving settlers claimed that God was punishing them for drunkenness and other sins.

Whether or not specific superstitions were tied to religious faith, most called for people to behave in certain ways, either to avoid bad luck or unwanted occurrences or to enjoy good luck or beneficial outcomes. One made sure, for instance, that a black cat did not cross one's path because if it did, bad luck would supposedly ensue. In contrast, Swedish settlers believed that good luck would come to those who, while selling a healthy cow, kept a wad of the animal's hair on their farm. Another favorable situation was no rain during harvest time; many settlers held that this could be ensured by saying the Lord's Prayer backward. Other common folk beliefs in various parts of the colonies said that people born during the first three days of each new year were fated to endure unhappy lives; and that if someone tripped over an abandoned grave, one of his or her relatives would soon die.

A great many other superstitions were inspired by astrology, particularly those connected to the moon. According to scholar David F. Hawke:

Farmers sowed and harvested crops, pruned fruit trees, slaughtered hogs, cut firewood, or built fences according to the phases of the moon. Moon watching was serious business for all. . . . A sampling of the [moon-related] lore . . . reveals that pole beans should be planted when the horns of the moon are up, [but] a farmer must not roof a building then, for the shingles will warp upward. He should plant root crops during the "dark of the moon" but not pick apples. . . . During a full moon a slaughtered cow will give juicy meat and a weaned calf will become a good milker; during a waning moon the farmer should cut timber, split firewood, and gather fruit and artichokes, but horses born in this phase will remain weak through life.[33]

Magical Practices and Cures

The line separating superstition from magic can sometimes be a fuzzy one, and this was certainly true in colonial times. For the sake of convenience, one could define magic in that era as using objects or words thought to possess special powers to bring about a desired outcome. Thus, a necromancer might cast a spell on someone with the intent of making him or her get sick or die. Or conversely, someone might employ magical objects or spells to cure sick people.

Belief in magic was widespread in Europe in late medieval times, especially

54 Religious Beliefs in Colonial America

Clergymen stand in the doorway of a sick woman's home. Colonists practiced more white magic than black magic, which was used to ward off or eradicate illness.

among the poor and uneducated. So when Europeans began colonizing other continents, including North America, some of them brought that belief with them. Each new immigrant group that settled in British America had its own peculiar ideas about magic. Those of the Germans who settled in Pennsylvania were the subject of condemnations by a Lutheran minister, Henry M. Muhlenberg, in the 1740s and 1750s. He felt that the colony had "more necromancers than Christians." The heads of too many of them, he claimed, "are full of fantastic notions of witchcraft and satanic arts," including "exorcism of devils."[34]

But as near as scholars can tell, far more colonists practiced so-called white, or beneficial, magic than black magic. The most common use for white magic was to either ward off or eradicate illness. Various objects were thought to possess magical properties under certain conditions. Tying a piece of red cloth around the head, for instance, was said by some to relieve severe headaches. And sliding a piece of metal, such as a knife blade or pair of scissors, down one's back supposedly stopped a nosebleed. Particularly widespread was belief in the magic properties of certain numbers, 3 and its multiple, 9, being the most common. One of several approaches was to repeat some step in the cure three times. It was also common to hide magical objects inside walls, chimneys, floors, roofs, and other household spaces to ward off disease. In addition, white magic was frequently employed to counteract black magic; for this task people often swore by a potion made from a root called wall fern.

Fear of Witches

Often associated with magic, especially the black kind, were witches, who could be either female or male (although female ones were thought to be more numerous). Fear of witches in colonial America is today mainly associated with the famous Salem witch trials in Massachusetts. However, terror of witches and other evil spirits, along with violence against people accused of witchcraft, actually occurred throughout the colonies in their first century.

Typical was an incident that occurred aboard a ship bound for Maryland in 1654. According to a Catholic Jesuit priest onboard, the vessel was caught in a terrible storm that lasted longer than most others, and

> the opinion arose that it [the storm] was not raised by the violence of the sea or atmosphere, but was occasioned by the malevolence [evil] of witches. Forthwith, they [the crew] seize[d] a little old woman suspected of sorcery, and after examining her with the strictest scrutiny, guilty or not guilty, they [killed] her [and] the corpse, and whatever belonged to her, they cast into the sea.[35]

Similarly, a Virginia woman named Virginia Sherwood was accused of practicing witchcraft in 1705. To prove she was guilty, the authorities applied the "dunking test," in which she was thrown into a pond. If she floated and lived, she was guilty, whereas if she sank and drowned, she was innocent, an obvious lose-lose proposition for the accused. Because of incomplete court records, Sherwood's fate remains unknown.

Where did such fears of old women with evil powers and/or ties to the devil come from? Like other forms of superstition, belief in witches began in Europe and came with early settlers to colonial America. The concept of witchcraft is very ancient. But persecution of witches did not become widespread until 1484, when Pope Innocent VIII issued an edict saying that witches were both real and a serious threat to godly people. At the time, most Europeans were devout Catholics and took the pope's words very seriously. As a result, the continent was engulfed by a wave of mass hysteria about witches. (Mass hysteria occurs when the members of a group all become convinced that something with no basis in fact is actually real.) During the next two centuries, an estimated 1 to 2 million people, mostly women, were brutally tortured and executed on suspicion of being witches.

The Salem Witches

By the late 1600s, Europe's massacre of witches had largely ended. But by that time, belief in and fear of witches had already spread to British America. And there the famous witch trials in Salem, Massachusetts, proved to be one of the last gasps of Western civilization's terror-ridden obsession with witches.

In retrospect the trials and the events surrounding them, which took place in the early 1690s, represent one of the most disturbing and best-documented cases of mass hysteria in history. Several

Witch trials began in Salem, Massachusetts, in the late 1600s. Some of the girls on trial were seen having "fits," leading others to believe the girls had been manipulated by witches.

Wracked with Guilt

People today who look back at the witch hunts and trials in Salem in the 1690s are often perplexed about why the young girls who accused others of being witches had seizurelike fits and other strange physical symptoms. To some degree, modern experts suspect, the girls were wracked with guilt. To combat boredom, and also out of innocent curiosity, they had been secretly playing games that included white magic. This turned out to be a serious mistake, for Puritan children were regularly and thoroughly programmed to believe in and fear the devil, demons, witches, and other supernatural beings. And they often heard lectures and sermons telling of dire consequences for anyone who even so much as told a lie, much less dabbled in magic or other practices associated with witches. Typical was this warning by Puritan leader Cotton Mather in one of his children's books:

They which lie [and commit other such offenses] must go to their father, the devil, into everlasting burning; they which never pray, God will pour out his wrath upon them; and when they bed and pray in hell fire, God will not forgive them, but there [they] must lie forever. Are you willing to go to hell and burn with the devil and his [evil] angels?

Modern medical experts have demonstrated that such fear-based indoctrination can cause some people to display debilitating physical symptoms.

Quoted in Rachel Walker, "Cotton Mather," Salem Witch Trials, Spring 2001. www.iath.virginia.edu/salem/people/c_mather.html.

young girls who lived in Salem, among them Elizabeth Parris and Abigail Williams, began having weird, seizurelike fits. The consensus of modern researchers is that these resulted from a combination of two factors. First, those aspects of the fits that were real came from the extreme guilt the girls felt for secretly playing games involving white magic, which were seen as terribly sinful in Puritan society. Second, gnawing anxiety that their parents would find out drove the girls to lie repeatedly to cover themselves. And to back up the lies, they faked at least some, if not most, of the seizures.

Whatever the actual causes of the fits, many grown-ups in the town concluded that the girls had been manipulated by witches. Several people were accused of witchcraft and brought to trial. Included in the so-called evidence used to prove that the accused were evil creatures was their inability to recite the Lord's Prayer without error. Supposedly, no witch or other agent of the devil could do so. Also acceptable as evidence was an accusation that someone was a witch made by a person who confessed to being a witch himself or herself. This was based on the notion that all witches knew or recognized one another. Spectral evidence was also allowed in court. This consisted of claims made by the young girls and others that they had seen specters, or invisible beings, attacking or harassing them.

In addition, the court permitted certain kinds of physical proof that someone was a witch. Authorities took the accused into a room, stripped the person naked, and examined his or her body. If they found a small red circle, called the "mark of the devil," on the skin, then the person was a witch. They might also administer a "pin test" by sticking the red mark with a pin. If no blood appeared, they concluded that the person was an agent of the devil.

On such feeble, superstitious "evidence," more and more people, including several men, were accused and convicted of being witches. Hundreds were thrown in jail and twenty, including a minister, were executed, mainly by hanging. Moreover, these executions were carried out with extreme cruelty. The convicted person was bound, taken to a hill near the town, and dragged up a ladder, where a noose was place around her or his neck. Then the executioner pushed the ladder away. In most cases, the victim's body did not drop with enough force to break the neck; so he or she slowly strangled to death. A victim's face turned "dark red from the dammed up blood that wept from eyes, nose, and mouth," explains one modern expert. "Starved lungs rasped loudly for the air they could no longer breathe. The whole body thrashed against its bonds as it convulsed uncontrollably, clenching and unclenching in every part.... After a last jerk, the body stilled, empty of life at last."[36]

Even after the person was dead, the display of meanness and brutality continued. Some men cut the body down and threw it into a shallow grave on the hillside. No prayers were said, no marker was placed on the grave, and no one was allowed to stay and pay their respects.

Accusing the Wrong People

The witch hunt in Salem went on until October 1692, at which point about 150 accused people languished in jail. At least another two hundred people suspected or accused of being witches had not yet been arrested because the local jails were full. Besides the charge against them, one thing that all of these unfortunate individuals had in common was that they were members of the lower classes. Indeed, the vast majority of those accused of witchcraft were poor or of modest means.

What suddenly caused this situation to change was that the afflicted girls began accusing members of the upper, ruling class of being witches. Among them was the wife of the governor of the colony. Not only were none of these high-ranking persons accused or arrested,

The Roots of Fear

Fear of witches in the colonies had its main roots in late medieval Europe. When Pope Innocent VIII proclaimed in 1484 that witches were real and that they should be feared and resisted, millions of people took heed. The few who made the mistake of using reason and expressing doubt about the reality of witchcraft were labeled heretics and either shunned or tortured. Steadfastly supporting the pope's pronouncement about witches, German monks James Sprenger and Heinrich Kramer published the *Malleus Maleficarum,* or *Witches' Hammer,* in 1486. It cataloged the various evil acts supposedly performed by witches and warned that witches ruined crops, kidnapped and ate children, and caused disease epidemics. Most Europeans of that era assumed that anything written by monks and approved by the pope must be true. So few questioned the authors' obvious hatred of women, narrow-mindedness, twisted sexual obsessions, or lack of human compassion. In the decades and centuries that followed, millions of women (along with a few men) were hunted down, brutalized, and/or killed, and some of this antiwitch mania eventually spilled over into the American colonies.

MALLEVS
MALEFICARVM,
MALEFICAS ET EARVM
hæresim frameâ conterens,

EX VARIIS AVCTORIBVS COMPILATVS,
& in quatuor Tomos iustè distributus;

QVORVM DVO PRIORES VANAS DÆMONVM
versutias, praestigiosas eorum delusiones, superstitiosas Strigimagarum
cæremonias, horrendos etiam cum illis congressus; exactam denique
tam pestiferæ sectæ disquisitionem, & punitionem complectuntur.
Tertius praxim Exorcistarum ad Dæmonum, & Strigimagarum male-
ficia de Christi fidelibus pellenda; Quartus verò Artem Doctrinalem,
Benedictionalem, & Exorcismalem continent.

TOMVS PRIMVS.
Indices Auctorum, capitum, rerùmque non desunt.

Editio nouissima, infinitis penè mendis expurgata; cuique accessit Fuga
Dæmonum & Complementum artis exorcisticæ.

Vir sive mulier, in quibus Pythonicus, vel diuinationis fuerit spiritus, morte moriatur
Leuitici cap. 10.

LVGDVNI,
Sumptibus CLAVDII BOVRGEAT, sub signo Mercurij Galli.

M. DC. LXIX.
CVM PRIVILEGIO REGIS.

Published in 1486, Witches' Hammer *described a variety of evil acts performed by witches.*

Known as the Salem Witch House, the home of Judge Jonathan Corwin is the only remaining structure in Salem with direct ties to the witchcraft trials of 1692.

but the authorities also immediately shut down the trials and executions. In addition, the governor ordered that no more people could be imprisoned on suspicion of witchcraft.

Years later a few of those whose lies had touched off the episode of mass delusion and needless bloodshed in Salem admitted their guilt and apologized. But this proved too little, too late. The lives of hundreds of people and dozens of families had been ruined. Of the several lessons learned from the Salem tragedy, one is that both superstition and religious belief were extremely powerful forces in colonial America. As such, under the right circumstances, they could explode, unleashing fear, paranoia, misery, and death. Another lesson that emerged was the reaffirmation of a fact of life in all human societies, past and present. Namely, only in a few historical times and places have ordinary folk successfully challenged the position of the rich, privileged, and powerful ruling classes. And colonial America was not one of those times and places.

Fringe Beliefs and Superstitions 61

Chapter Five

RELIGION AND
SCIENCE IN ALLIANCE

In the modern world, the vast majority of religious leaders do not also claim to be scientists. And most scientists stick mainly to studying and promoting scientific ideas and rarely involve themselves in religious arguments or try to reconcile science with religion. As a result, most people consider science and religion as separate disciplines (though overlap and/or conflicts between them do sometimes occur).

The situation was quite different in colonial America, however. There, the religious and scientific worlds came together in a sort of alliance forged by the leading educated persons of the day. At the time, what people today call science was still in its formative stages. The most common term for it was *natural philosophy* (sometimes also called "natural history"). The vast majority of highly educated colonists (who were mostly

men) were religiously devout, and in fact a large percentage of them were ministers. Yet almost to a man they were fascinated by natural philosophy. And it was common among them to devote many hours each week to studying, discussing, or writing about such topics as botany, zoology, anatomy, geology, astronomy, optics, and mathematics.

No less important than these men's interest and expertise in science was the fact that they did not see it as an obstacle or threat to their religious beliefs. Indeed, they came to view the ideal citizen and leader as one who studied both religion and science and found ways to reconcile them so that one supported the other. One of the leading minister-scientists of the era, Cotton Mather, ably summed it up, saying, "A blessed land was New England, when there was over part of it a governor who was not only a Christian and a gentleman, but also an eminent philosopher [scientist]."[37] (The governor to which he refers is John Winthrop the Younger of Connecticut, an avid science buff.) Mather wrote *The Christian Philosopher* (1721), a book whose title perfectly captures the spirit of the religious-scientific partnership that characterized the age.

Intellectual Influences

The strong interest in science of so many in the colonial educated classes did not develop in a vacuum. Rather, it was an outgrowth of an ongoing transformation of ideas and knowledge that was already occurring in Europe during the years when the first North American colonies were founded. That transformation, which

Minister-scientist Cotton Mather was the author of The Christian Philosopher.

An Exhaustive Look at the Natural Order

The following synopsis of Cotton Mather's book The Christian Philosopher *was published in the May 2009 issue of the journal* Theology and Science.

Cotton Mather was few things if not thorough. The perspective he adopted in *The Christian Philosopher* was exhaustive in scope. The work's thirty-five chapters cover the full range of the created order. Mather began with light and moved to the stars, the planets, and comets before turning to terrestrial matters. He considered all possible forms of precipitation—rain, snow, hail—and he observed the general properties of fluids. He then considered organic life: vegetables, insects, reptiles, fish, birds, and four-footed mammals. Finally, his last and longest chapter by nearly two-fold was that on humans. Interspersed in these chapters are reflections on the laws of physics: heat, magnetism, and gravity. On the one hand, Mather addressed creation in roughly the same order as that of the first chapter of Genesis. However, on a more systematic level, Mather presented a progression from the least to the most human. The significance of all this is that Mather considered all possible manifestations of nature, from the most faintly discernible law of physics to the lowliest form of organic life, in his endeavor to understand the natural world and humanity's place in it.

George Faithful, "Cotton Mather's Scientific Method for Prayer," *Theology and Science*, May 2009, pp. 177–78.

spanned the 1600s and 1700s, was spearheaded by an intellectual movement eventually dubbed the European Enlightenment. Most of its principal thinkers were French and especially English. So it is not surprising that its concepts were readily absorbed in England's American colonies.

Some of the ideas generated by the Enlightenment were related to religious toleration, human rights, and efficient and fair government. But many others encompassed the rising tide of science, which was changing the way people viewed the world and universe around them. One of the main tenets of the new worldview was that nature operates by comprehensible, measurable scientific principles. For that reason, natural forces and events can be understood through the application of reason, observation, experimentation, and logical deduction.

This new way of looking at the universe did not necessarily exclude God and religion from the discussion. In fact, a number of Enlightenment thinkers reconciled religion with science by suggesting the scientific laws of nature were

THE
Tvvoo Bookes of
FRANCIS BACON.

Of the proficience and aduance
ment of Learning, diuine and
humane.

To the King.

AT LONDON,
¶ Printed for *Henrie Tomes,* and
are to be fould at his fhop at Graies Inne
Gate in Holborne. 1605.

The Advancement of Learning *by Francis Bacon was admired by Enlightenment thinkers, ministers, teachers, and political leaders.*

actually God's special handiwork; they had long remained hidden, and humans were just now discovering them. This spirit of reconciliation was absorbed by educated colonists along with the more tangible, factual aspects of the Enlightenment.

Among the Enlightenment thinkers, one of the most influential in the American colonies was English lawyer and philosopher Francis Bacon (1561–1626). It is important to note that he was admired as much by ministers as by teachers and political leaders, all of whom were interested in science. Particularly popular among these educated colonists was Bacon's 1605 treatise *The Advancement of Learning*. In it he provides a detailed classification for existing knowledge, with three main headings—history, poetry, and philosophy (including what is today called science)—with several subtopics under each. He also dismisses or condemns magic and astrology as false belief systems; extolls the virtues of learning and values of reason; and promotes the idea that all worthwhile knowledge is rooted in the laws of nature.

Science and Religion in School

Thanks to the importance placed on learning by Bacon and other intellectuals of his and the following generation, many colonial American leaders advocated the creation of schools of higher learning. The two general realms of knowledge they most revered were reli-

gion and science. So the early colleges established in the colonies were designed to turn out graduates who were well versed in both. A high proportion of graduates became ministers, although some entered other fields.

The first advanced educational institution of this type in the colonies was Harvard College, founded near Boston in 1636. Within a few years of its opening, it offered courses in logic, mathematics, as-

Harvard College was the first advanced educational institution to combine religious and scientific studies.

tronomy, botany, and physics in addition to its strong religious curriculum. Thus, all of the young men who graduated from the school and became preachers in churches throughout the colonies carried with them a deep respect for and impressive knowledge of scientific disciplines.

Some of these ministers fondly remembered studying under one of Harvard's most famous professors, John Winthrop IV, great-grandson of the John Winthrop whom Mather had praised so highly. The later Winthrop began teaching at Harvard in 1738 and became a

Religion and Science in Alliance   67

model of the educated colonial man; among those he directly inspired was Benjamin Franklin, one of the greatest minds, as well as reconcilers of science and religion, of the day. One of Winthrop's first steps after taking the job at Harvard "was to procure a copy of [Isaac] Newton's *Principia*, which became his guide," writes Louis B. Wright, a noted scholar of colonial times. According to Wright:

> Friends in England sent Winthrop books and "philosophical apparatus" [scientific instruments], including a telescope which had belonged to [astronomer] Edmund Halley, after whom a spectacular comet was named. Said to have been the first to teach Newton's fluxions (calculus), Winthrop stimulated a fresh interest in mathematics, theoretical speculation, and [scientific] investigation. . . . With the progress made by Winthrop at Harvard, academic training in science came of age in [America].[38]

Like other learned colonists of his day, Winthrop tried to reconcile religion and

Ticks and Biting Horse Flies

William Byrd II, a devout Christian, had a strong interest in science. In 1728 he took part in a major survey of the North Carolina backcountry, and in a journal that he kept of the trip, he jotted down his observations of the insects of the region. Byrd writes:

And now [that] I am upon the subject of insects, it may not be improper to mention some few remedies against those that are most vexatious in this climate. The ticks are either deer-ticks, or those that annoy the cattle. The first kind are long, and take a very strong grip, being most in remote woods, above the inhabitants. The other are round, and more gently insinuate themselves into the flesh, being in all places where cattle are frequent. . . . The horse flies are not only a great grievance to horses, but likewise to those that ride them. [Although] this insect be no bigger than an ordinary fly, it bites very smartly. . . . Bears' oil is used by the Indians as a general defense against every species of vermin. Among the rest, they say it keeps both bugs and mosquitoes from assaulting their persons, which would otherwise devour such uncleanly people, [but] the remedy was worse than the disease.

William Byrd, *The Westover Manuscripts: Containing the History of the Dividing Line Betwixt Virginia and North Carolina*. Petersburg, VA: Edmund and Julius C. Ruffin, 1841. www.learnnc.org/lp/editions/nchist-colonial/4116.

science. A classic example is his reaction to the great earthquake that leveled Lisbon, Portugal, in 1755. While a majority of people across the world were sure that the disaster was a divine punishment, he describes it as a scientifically explainable natural event that God likely took advantage of to make a moral statement.

Other colleges and professors in the colonies eventually followed Harvard's and Winthrop's lead in creating a balance between religious and scientific knowledge. Virginia's College of William and Mary, Connecticut's Yale, New Jersey's Princeton, and New York's Columbia all originally featured religious instruction. But they also offered an array of scientific courses.

Informal Science Educations

Distinguished college professors like John Winthrop and their students were not the only colonists who embraced science and easily reconciled it with their religious beliefs. In addition to those who learned about science in formal academic settings, there were many others who educated themselves informally by various means. For example, several upper-class individuals, whether or not they attended college, bought as many books as they could, both old and new, on scientific subjects. And in this way they built up extensive home libraries. One was John Winthrop the Younger, who possessed the largest collection of science books in British America at the time of his death in 1676. Throughout

his adult life he freely lent these volumes to fellow devotees of natural philosophy living in several different colonies. This helped to spread scientific knowledge to many Americans who owned books about religion but not about science. Cotton Mather, who so highly praised Winthrop as a gentleman-scholar, also possessed an impressive private library that was the largest in the colonies in the year of his own death (1728). A large proportion of Mather's books were on scientific subjects.

Another way that knowledge of science spread was through colonists' own observations, studies, experiments, and writings. Some twenty-five colonial Americans became members of England's prestigious scientific organization, the Royal Society. And they periodically sent data and specimens they had collected to members of that organization both in Europe and the colonies.

One of these individuals was Virginia's William Byrd II (1674–1744), a well-to-do plantation owner. A staunchly religious Anglican, he believed that God could and did intervene in human affairs. In his popular work, *The Commonplace Book*, he writes:

> Almost every act of Providence [God] is an instance of compassion to mankind and even the terrors of God's justice are instruments of his love, to affright us from our sins and make us capable of his mercy. To this purpose, it's remarkable that when our sins are great enough to

draw down a plague upon a city or nation, it first strikes the cattle before it reaches mankind, that they may, by so near and so visible a warning, have time to humble themselves and sue [beg] for pardon.[39]

It is noteworthy that Byrd's comments about disease afflicting cattle before humans is a scientific observation he felt was important enough to include in a major religious statement. Indeed, like other educated colonists, he often used scientific concepts to support religious ones. Meanwhile, to quench his thirst for scientific knowledge, he often jotted down information about animals, plants, rocks and minerals, and other natural phenomena he encountered in his travels in the mid-Atlantic colonies. In 1728 he observed alligators in North Carolina's Santee River and made a journal entry that reads in part:

England's presitigious scientific organization, the Royal Society, was formed at Gresham College in London.

A small kind of alligator is frequently seen, which perfumes the water with a musky smell. They seldom exceed eight feet in length in these parts. . . . The heat of the climate does not only make them bigger, but more fierce and voracious [hungry]. They watch the cattle there when they come to drink and cool themselves in the river. . . . However, as fierce and as strong as these monsters are, the Indians will surprise them napping as they float upon the surface, get astride upon their necks, then whip a short piece of wood like a truncheon [club] into their jaws, and holding the ends with their two hands, hinder them from diving by keeping their mouths open, and when they are almost spent, they will make to the shore, where their riders knock them on the head and eat them.[40]

Byrd also wrote informal but detailed scientific papers for the Royal Society, including one titled "An Account of a Negro Boy That is Dappled in Several Places of His Body with White Spots."

Cotton Mather on God's Handiwork

Even more prolific in writing about both religion and science was the New England Puritan minister Cotton Mather (1663–1728). Contrary to popular belief, the Puritans, though extremely religiously devout, were not against science. (Two factors give that impression: First, most Puritans believed in witches, a very unscientific concept; second, many people today mistakenly assume that everyone who lived in past eras accepted either religion or science, not both.)

In fact, the Puritans were enthusiastic promoters of learning. They also embraced both Copernican astronomy (which advocated that earth revolves around the sun, not the other way around), and Newtonian physics (Isaac Newton's laws of motion and gravity). To Puritans like Mather, these recently discovered scientific ideas were not refutations of traditional religion. Rather, they were proof that God had created elegant natural laws to set the universe in motion. And Newton and other leading scientists had merely been smart enough to uncover God's natural handiwork.

These themes, strongly reconciling religion and science, pervade many of Mather's numerous writings. Like other highly educated colonists, he was strongly influenced by Bacon and other Enlightenment thinkers. Mather was particularly partial to Irish chemist and gentleman scientist Robert Boyle (1627–1691). In his *The Usefulness of Experimental Natural Philosophy* (1663), as well as in other works, Boyle argues that natural phenomena of all kinds, including the laws of nature (now called the laws of physics), are logical constructs or designs created by God.

Inspired by such ideas, Mather concluded that if God worked through natural, scientific forces, the events described

Irish chemist Robert Boyle argued that natural phenomena of all kinds are logical constructs or designs created by God.

in the Bible could be interpreted in scientific as well as religious terms. So he wrote a treatise titled *Biblio Americana*, in which he uses known scientific principles to explain various biblical incidents. Among these principles is the then-tentative atomic theory of matter (which states that all things are made up of tiny particles called atoms). One passage from the book reads:

In the beginning was universal matter by God first created of nothing; a wondrous [mixture] of all sort of [atomic] particles, unformed and unmoved and everywhere separated from one another with empty spaces. This universal matter was put into motion, by the spirit of God, and not left unto fortuitous [accidental or random] motion and

Winthrop at the Epicenter

Harvard professor John Winthrop's reputation as a rational scientist and expert on earthquakes stemmed from more than his commentary on the terrible Lisbon earthquake of November 1, 1755. Just seventeen days later, on November 18, the American colonies were hit by the worst quake of the colonial era. Known as the Cape Ann Earthquake (or Boston Earthquake), it could be felt as far away as Nova Scotia in the north and the Carolinas in the south. Winthrop lived near the epicenter of the quake, and he analyzed the aftereffects in his own home. One modern observer explains:

By measuring effects, he carefully deduced the chronology and characteristics of the shock, applying physical maxims whenever he could. He documented the existence of both horizontal and vertical motion during a tremor, comparing the generation of earthquake "waves" to that of the vibrations of a struck musical chord, where an instrument's strings bend broadly at first and then vibrate increasingly rapidly in returning to their stationary positions. . . . To determine the speed of the sway of the region's buildings in the earthquake, he relied on the travels of a key tossed from his mantel and measured the distance that one of his chimney bricks had been thrown—thirty feet from a thirty-two-foot-high chimney. By calibrating the known speed of a falling object . . . he could show that his brick had probably traveled twenty-one feet in one second. The clue of the key, which had apparently not traveled so forcefully, suggested to him that the velocity of moving objects during an earthquake varied, depending on height.

Jourdan Houston, "The Great Earthquake," American Heritage.com. www.americanheritage.com/articles/maga zine/ ah/1980/5/1980_5_102.shtml.

The worst earthquake of the colonial era, the Cape Ann Earthquake, had its epicenter in Gloucester, Massachusetts.

concourse. Thus, was there given unto matter that force which we call nature; for nature is nothing but that motion which the spirit of God has imprinted upon matter, and which He perpetually governs with his infinite wisdom.[41]

Mather also produced writings that ably summarize and explain some of the major scientific concepts of his day. In *The Christian Philosopher*, for instance, he includes a section containing largely correct concepts about the stars and other heavenly bodies. Describing it, scholar Bruce Kirk Oldfield writes:

Mather [correctly] says that the number of stars one can count depends on the magnification of the telescope; that the Milky Way is made of an infinite number of stars; and that the universe is a three-dimensional object. He also states in his essays on stars that the constellations and stars should be renamed with Christian names. In subsequent essays on the sun and planets Mather includes descriptions of [German astronomer Johannes] Kepler's laws of planetary motions and the universality of physical laws and constants. [Also included are] several tables on planetary distances from the Sun, planetary diameters and their periods of revolution.[42]

In retrospect, although Mather, the Winthrops, Byrd, and other learned colonists were all religious men, they were not intellectual conservatives. In other words, they did not see new ideas about the universe as threats to religion. Nor did they rigidly maintain and defend older interpretations of religious doctrine. Instead, they were liberal, or progressive, thinkers who viewed newly discovered natural laws as part of a universal fabric God had designed. As a result, a favorable attitude toward science developed in early America. This would prove to be one of several factors that placed the United States in the forefront of worldwide progress in science and technology.

Chapter Six

RELIGION AND THE AMERICAN REVOLUTION

Fortunately for the citizenry of England's North American colonies, religion was not one of the causes of the American Revolution. In prior decades and centuries, Europe and other parts of the world had witnessed numerous conflicts fought mainly or in part over religious differences. But a war of that sort was unthinkable in colonial America in the mid-to-late 1700s. The simple reason was that more religious diversity, freedom, and tolerance existed in the colonies in that era than anywhere else on the planet. True, the many and varied colonial faiths did recognize that they had certain differences. But no one felt any need to fight over them.

Nevertheless, religious views did come into play in a number of ways in the decades leading up to the Revolution, as well as during and after it. Some American religious groups were less enthusiastic about the idea of separating from the mother country than others, for example. Also, religion helped shape the mindset of the so-called founding fathers—the leading architects of the Revolution and the new nation it produced, among them George Washington, Thomas Jefferson, and James Madison. Their peculiar religious views profoundly affected the nature of their blueprint for that new nation, the U.S. Constitution. And in turn, the Constitution's approach to religion, then unique in the world, guaranteed that the religious diversity and tolerance that had existed in America before the great rebellion would endure in the centuries that followed it.

Some Thorny Religious Issues

Thanks to the extraordinary diversity and tolerance among the various colonial religious groups, they rarely spoke out

Jonathan Mayhew, a Boston minister, spoke against having Anglican bishops in the colony.

against one another in the years directly preceding the Revolution. However, they did sometimes oppose outside influences they saw as threatening. And resentment over such influences helped to intensify the anti-British feelings that eventually led to armed rebellion.

Perhaps the best-known example is what many colonists came to call the "bishop question." During the colonies' early decades, their Anglican citizens had made it abundantly clear they did not want English bishops telling them what to do. So colonial churches long remained bishop free. That same thorny issue resurfaced in the 1750s and 1760s, however. Rumors that a bishop might be appointed inspired a Boston minister, Jonathan Mayhew, to rail against the idea in his sermons. Repeatedly he used the word *tyranny* to describe supposed attempts by Anglican officials in England to impose their will on Anglican colonists.

Arguments over the issue became even more heated in 1761. A haughty Anglican preacher in Cambridge, just outside of Boston, built himself a large mansion, which raised a great deal of suspicion. Many people worried that it was part of a plan to install an English bishop who would, in one writer's words, "destroy religious liberty, convene [church] courts to try colonists for religious offenses, and use government funds to promote Anglican causes."[43]

Although no bishop was ever appointed in Cambridge, the bishop question continued to be raised in New England and New York in the years that followed. In the early 1770s, with anti-British sentiments rising over unfair taxation and other political issues, a number of colonists began believing a nasty rumor that Catholics and English Anglicans were plotting to destroy religious freedom in the colonies. In 1774 Boston silversmith and engraver Paul Revere, who had become a radical anti-British patriot, exploited the rumor. He drew a cartoon showing a group of Anglican bishops and members of Parliament meeting with the devil to plan a takeover of colonial churches.

Fears that Anglican or Catholic bishops would impose tyrannical rule over freedom-loving colonists proved groundless. But the loyalty of many Anglican colonists to the British monarchy was quite real. During the American Revolution, large numbers of colonists did remain loyal to the crown, and a hefty proportion of them were Anglicans. This is not surprising, since the English king was the head of the Anglican Church, or Church of England. And many Anglican colonists felt torn between loyalty to their country and loyalty to their faith. Either way, the result was a certain amount of resentment toward Anglicans by members of other faiths during the war.

Still another religious theme that cropped up during the Revolutionary period was a belief in some quarters that the war had a deeper meaning, one rooted in Christianity. Some ministers preached that the colonies' separation from Britain and formation of the United States was the signal for the coming of Jesus Christ's kingdom on earth. Throughout history, such predictors of Christ's return have been called, among other things, millennialists. (The term *millennialism* derives from the word *millennium*, meaning a thousand years; such predictors usually claim that upon returning to earth, Christ will reign for a thousand years.)

In 1776 a Connecticut preacher, Ebenezer Baldwin, told his parishioners that Jesus would reappear at any moment, and the new nation the patriots were establishing would become "the principal seat of that glorious Kingdom, which Christ shall erect upon the Earth in the latter days."[44] A majority of Americans rejected such notions. Yet millennialist fervor during the Revolution became part of a larger pattern in later American religious thought in which some people continued to claim that God favors America.

Nature's God

Such issues as the bishop question and millennialism ended up having no measurable effect on the waging and outcome of the American Revolution. However, other aspects of religion did affect the formation, laws, and values of the new nation that emerged from that momentous insurrection. One such aspect consisted of the spiritual beliefs of the founding fathers and the role they saw for religion in society.

A clue to the beliefs a number of the founders held appears in the Declaration of Independence, penned by Thomas Jefferson. In that famous document, Jefferson mentions "the laws of nature and of nature's God."[45] The term *nature's God* refers to the god of the deists. Many of the founders were traditional Christians, including Anglicans and Congregationalists. George Washington, for example, was an Anglican. But a fair number were deists, among them Jefferson, Benjamin Franklin, James Madison, and Thomas Paine.

It is important to emphasize that many of the deists of that era were Christians who incorporated various points of

deist thinking into their worldview. Some leading patriots, including John Adams, were Unitarians. These men agreed with the deists on some points and disagreed with them on others. Deism, one of several offshoots of the European Enlightenment, emerged in England in the early 1600s. It is not a separate denomination, but rather a particular point of view adopted by Christians of various existing denominations. As one modern observer describes it:

> deism has no church and no official organization, hence, it is not considered a religion. It is more a reason-based view of religion in general. Deism is sometimes referred to as a religious philosophy or a religious outlook. In general, Deism did not see Christ as the Son of God, did not believe in the Trinity, had no strong belief in miracles, and had no belief in atonement or resurrection.[46]

What deists view as miraculous are the intricacy and innate beauty of the laws of nature, which they believe God created. In the words of the great modern historian Will Durant:

> the real revelation [of deism] is in nature herself, and in man's God-given reason. The real God is the God that [Isaac] Newton revealed, the designer of a marvelous world operating majestically according to invariable [natural] law, and the

Of the founders who accepted deism, Thomas Jefferson was among its strongest supporters.

A Call for Avoiding War

During the increasing political, social, and military tensions in the years immediately preceding the American Revolution, ministers in some religious groups worried that a war with Britain would destroy the colonies. So in their sermons they preached caution and suggested ways of making amends with the mother country. In a letter to the faithful drafted in May 1775, Presbyterian leaders said:

It is well known to you . . . that we have not been instrumental in inflaming the minds of the people or urging them to acts of violence and disorder. . . . We think it of importance, at this time, to recommend to all of every rank [social class], but especially to those who may be called to action, a spirit of humanity and mercy. Every battle of the warrior is with confused noise, and garments rolled in blood. It is impossible to appeal to the sword without being exposed to many scenes of cruelty and slaughter. But it is often observed that civil wars are carried on with a rancor and spirit of revenge. . . . We conclude with our most earnest prayer that the God of heaven may bless you [and] that the present unnatural dispute may be speedily terminated by an equitable and lasting settlement on constitutional principles.

Quoted in Presbyterian Board of Publication, *Records of the Presbyterian Church in the United States of America, 1706–1788.* Philadelphia, PA: Presbyterian Board of Publication, 1904, pp. 467, 469.

real morality is the life of reason in harmony with nature.[47]

Of the founders who were deists, Jefferson and Paine were among the strongest supporters of the deist point of view.

Separation of Church and State

Deists like Jefferson tended to be even more religiously tolerant than the non-deist founders, who were themselves extraordinarily tolerant men. The result was that, compared to leaders in other nations, all of the U.S. founders were unusually respectful and inclusive of the beliefs of all citizens, including Christians, non-Christians, and even nonbelievers. In addition, these men were suspicious and disapproving of the strong hold that various religions exerted over the governments of many nations. In their view, no single religion should exert control over a government, if it did, history had repeatedly shown, sooner or later the freedom of and tolerance for other faiths would be threatened.

For these reasons, in structuring the government of the new nation, the founders made sure there would be no established (state-sponsored or state-supported) religion. Jefferson recalls how, in 1779, well before the U.S. Constitution was created, he and his fellow Virginia legislators dealt with the same issue while drafting the *Virginia Act for Establishing Religious Freedom*. Those who wanted to make Christianity the state religion were in the minority, and the majority overruled them for fear of alienating people of other faiths. Jefferson explains:

> Where the preamble declares that coercion [forcing people to believe a certain way] is a departure from the plan of the holy author of our religion, an amendment was proposed [to insert] "Jesus Christ," so that it would read "A departure from the plan of Jesus Christ, the holy author of our religion." The insertion was rejected by the great majority [of legislators because they wanted to include] within the mantle of [the law's] protection, the Jew and the Gentile, the Christian and Muslim, the Hindu and Infidel of every denomination.[48]

Later in 1789, when tackling the issue of religious freedom for the U.S. Constitution, the founders were equally careful to be fair and inclusive. To ensure religious freedom for all, they set up a government in which church and state are separate. The document's First Amendment reads in part, "Congress shall make no law respecting an establishment of religion, or prohibiting the free exercise thereof."[49] Noted scholar Jon Butler points out that this eminently wise and far-thinking statement

> looked in two directions simultaneously. It confirmed the diverse and vigorous religious expressions created in the colonial period and guaranteed that government would not engage in religious activity itself. For the future, it freed religion from government, and government from religion, in unprecedented ways never proposed by any society, Old World or New. Both paths . . . embodied the essence of colonial American religious development—the evolution of a lively, multifaceted, multiracial, multiethnic, religious world brought forth mainly by independent groups and individuals rather than by the state.[50]

At the time the new nation was established, few foreign nations understood America's government or its intentions. For all they knew, Jefferson, Washington, and their colleagues might be like many other national leaders who imposed their will and/or their religion on other peoples. The founders showed that they were different, in part through a statement made in the Treaty of Tripoli.

The Treaty of Tripoli was an agreement of friendship with the small North

African Muslim nation of Tripoli. It was initially drafted near the end of George Washington's first presidential term and ratified by the U.S. Senate in the first few months of John Adams's presidency. Article 11 of the treaty states:

> As the government of the United States of America is not in any sense founded on the Christian religion; as it has in itself no character of enmity against [opposition to] the laws, religion, or tranquility of Islam; and as the said states [nations] never have entered into any war or act of hostility against any Muslim nation, it is declared by the parties that no pretext arising from religious opinions shall ever produce an interruption of the harmony existing between the two countries.[51]

Today the wording of Article 11 of the Tripoli treaty is sometimes controversial and occasionally debated by both scholars and nonscholars. Some argue that the article is proof that the founders did not intend for the United States to be a Christian nation. Others disagree and say that the founders did view the nation as a Christian one. Still others point out that the article in question does not refer to the U.S. nation, but rather to the U.S. government. They say that an examination of original documents from that era, including letters and commentaries by the founders, suggests that they viewed the United States as a predominately Christian nation but felt that the government should neither advocate nor support any specific religion.

After Independence

Despite their insistence that church and state remain separate, the founders never lost sight of the important role religion played in their society. And neither did the majority of citizens of the new nation. True, during the war itself, a number of American religious groups suffered. Anglican churches lost a whopping 75 percent of their ministers, who, because they supported the king, had been harassed and chased away by local patriots. And a number of Anglican churches were vandalized. Baptist worship was often disrupted during the fighting and many of the faith's congregations disbanded. Meanwhile, Quaker groups were sharply split over the war; some held on to traditional Quaker principles of pacifism and urged patriots to lay down their arms, while others rejected this approach and supported the Revolution.

After the war, however, many American religious groups recovered and became just as strong and successful as they had been in colonial times and in some cases more so. Anglicans, Baptists, Methodists, Catholics, Jews, and many others increased in numbers in the decades following the Revolution. In their sermons, leaders of all faiths praised the soldiers who had fought for independence, rallied around the new government, and offered its leaders spiritual guidance.

The Roots of Deism

Darren Staloff, a professor of history at the City College of New York, provides this concise overview of the origins of deism.

Lord Edward Herbert of Cherbury, a prominent English statesman and thinker, laid out the basic Deist creed in [1624]. Herbert was reacting to the ongoing religious strife and bloodletting that had wracked Europe since the onset of the Reformation in the previous century. . . . Deism, Herbert hoped, would quell this strife by offering a rational and universal creed. [He] established the existence of God from the so-called cosmological argument that, since everything has a cause, God must be acknowledged as the first cause of the universe itself. Given the existence of God, it is our duty to . . . strive to be virtuous and expect punishment and reward in the afterlife. Because this creed was based on reason which was shared by all men [Herbert] hoped it would be acceptable to everyone regardless of their religious background. . . . Despite Herbert's efforts, Deism had very little impact in England for most of the 17th century. But in the years from 1690 to 1740, the very height of the Enlightenment in England, Deism became a major source of [discussion and] spread [to the American colonies. There, as in Europe, Deists formulated] the argument from design, namely that the clockwork order of the universe implied an intelligent designer, i.e. God the cosmic clockmaker. [But] unlike the God of Scripture, the Deist God was remarkably distant; after designing his clock, he simply wound it up and let it run. At the same time, his benevolence was evidenced by the astounding precision and beauty of his workmanship. Indeed, part of the attraction of Deism lay in its foisting a sort of cosmic optimism. . . . True Deist piety was moral behavior in keeping with the Golden Rule of benevolence.

Darren Staloff, "Deism and the Founding of the United States," National Humanities Center. http://nationalhumanitiescenter.org/tserve/eighteen/ekeyinfo/deism.htm.

Lord Edward Herbert of Cherbury was the founder of the deist movement.

At the same time, the creation of a new nation that granted a high degree of personal liberty to both individuals and groups further solidified the religious diversity that had developed in the colonies. As Butler puts it, the government's guarantees of religious freedom

recognized the extraordinary, almost unimaginable diversity of religion that emerged in colonial America, a spiritual pluralism unlike that found in any society on either side of the Atlantic or Pacific. It guaranteed that government would not itself seek to change that diversity by intervening in religion or by supporting one or more religious groups. . . . No other government in Western civilization had ever before made such pledges.[52]

Because of this remarkable governmental commitment to religious choice, today the United States is even more religiously diverse and tolerant than it was in colonial times. And this is one reason that America remains, as it was then, a powerful magnet for those seeking the freedom to think and worship as they please.

Notes

Introduction: From Religious Freedom to Religious Tolerance

1. Quoted in Rufus M. Jones, *The Quakers in the American Colonies*. London: Macmillan, 1923, p. 71.
2. Louis B. Wright, *The Cultural Life of the American Colonies, 1607–1763*. New York: Harper and Row, 2002, pp. 72–73.
3. Quoted in James A. Haught, *Holy Horrors*. New York: Prometheus, 1990, p. 94.
4. Library of Virginia, "Virginia Statute for Religious Freedom, 16 January 1786." www.lva.virginia.gov/lib-edu/ education/bor/ vsrftext.htm.

Chapter One: Native American Religious Beliefs

5. Carl Waldman, *Atlas of the North American Indian*. New York: Facts On File, 2009, p. 57.
6. Christine Leigh Heyrman, "Native American Religion in Early America," National Humanities Center. http://nationalhumanitiescenter.org/tserve/eighteen/ekeyinfo/natrel.htm.
7. Quoted in Frederick E. Hoxie, ed. *Encyclopedia of North American Indians*. Boston: MA: Houghton Mifflin, 1996, p. 539.
8. Quoted in Hoxie, "Religion," p. 540.
9. Washington Matthews, *Ethnology and Philology of the Hidatsa Indians*. Washington, DC: U.S. Geological and Geographical Survey, 1877, p. 49.
10. Quoted in Peter Farb, *Man's Rise to Civilization as Shown by the Indians of North America from Primeval Times to the Coming of the Industrial State*. New York: Penguin, 1991, p. 198.
11. Hartley B. Alexander, *The Mythology of All Races, Volume X: North American*. New York: Cooper Square, 1964, pp. xxiii–xxiv.
12. Quoted in Wilcomb E. Washburn, ed., *The Indian and the White Man*. Garden City, NY: Doubleday, 1964, p. 213.

Chapter Two: A Great Diversity of Faiths

13. Wright, *The Cultural Life of the American Colonies*. p. 72.
14. John Winthrop, "A Model of Christian Charity," The Religious Freedom Page. http://religiousfreedom.lib.virginia.edu/sacred/charity.html.
15. Jon Butler, *New World Faiths: Religion in Colonial America*. New York: Oxford University Press, 2007, p. 54.
16. John C. Miller, *The First Frontier: Life in Colonial America*. Lanham, MD: University Press of America, 1986, p. 266.
17. Edward G. Gray, *Colonial America: A*

History in Documents. New York: Oxford University Press, 2003, p. 131.

18. Quoted in Butler, *New World Faiths.* p. 72.

19. Charles Woodmason, "The Journal of Reverend Charles Woodmason," Teaching American History.org. http://teachingamericanhistory.org/library/index.asp? document=1068.

20. Charles Chauncy, "Charles Chauncy, Against Revivalism, August 4, 1742," Bible and History. www.piney.com/ChauncyRevivalism.html.

21. Quoted in Richard L. Bushman, *The Great Awakening, Documents on the Revival of Religion, 1740–1745.* Chapel Hill: University of North Carolina Press, 1969, pp. 51–52.

22. Louis B. Wright, *Everyday Life in Colonial America.* New York: Putnam's, 1965, pp. 94–95.

23. Olaudah Equiano, *The Interesting Narrative of the Life of Olaudah Equiano Written by Himself,* ed. Robert J. Allison. Boston, MA: Bedford, 1995, pp. 41–43.

24. Gray, *Colonial America,* p. 132.

Chapter Three: Clergymen, Worshippers, and Churches

25. Patricia U. Bonomi, *Under the Cope of Heaven: Religion, Society, and Politics in Colonial America.* New York: Oxford University Press, 2003, pp. 39–40.

26. Hugh Jones, *The Present State of Virginia,* ed. Richard L. Morton. Chapel Hill: University of North Carolina Press, 1956, p. 101.

27. Quoted in Bonomi, *Under the Cope of Heaven.* p. 55.

28. Bonomi, *Under the Cope of Heaven.* p. 69.

29. Quoted in George Leon Walker, *Some Aspects of the Religious Life of New England.* New York: Silver, Burnett, 1897. http://historymatters.gmu.edu/d/5711.

30. Bonomi, *Under the Cope of Heaven.* p. 107.

31. Butler, *New World Faiths.* p. 118.

Chapter Four: Fringe Beliefs and Superstitions

32. Gray, *Colonial America.* p. 137.

33. David F. Hawke, *Everyday Life in Early America.* New York: Harper and Row, 1989, pp. 159–160.

34. Quoted in Butler, *New World Faiths.* p. 86.

35. Quoted in Clayton C. Hall, ed., *Narratives of Early Maryland.* New York: Scribner's, 1910, p. 141.

36. Marilynne K. Roach, *The Salem Witch Trials: A Day-by-Day Chronicle of a Community Under Siege.* New York: Taylor Trade, 2002, p. 168.

Chapter Five: Religion and Science in Alliance

37. Cotton Mather, *Magnalia Christi Americana.* Hartford, CT: Silas Andrus, 1855, p. 159.

38. Wright, *The Cultural Life of the American Colonies.* p. 225.

39. William Byrd, *The Commonplace*

Book, ed. Kevin Berland et al. Chapel Hill: University of North Carolina Press, 2001, p. 169.

40. William Byrd, *The Westover Manuscripts: Containing the History of the Dividing Line Betwixt Virginia and North Carolina.* Petersburg, VA: Edmund and Julius C. Ruffin, 1841. www.learnnc.org/lp/editions/nchist-colonial/4116.

41. Quoted in Bruce Kirk Oldfield, "Science and Religion in Colonial America: The Early Days," Forum on Public Policy Online, Fall 2006. www.forumonpublicpolicy.com/archive06/oldfield.pdf.

42. Oldfield, "Science and Religion in Colonial America."

Chapter Six: Religion and the American Revolution

43. Butler, *New World Faiths.* p. 134.

44. Quoted in Paul Boyer, *When Time Shall Be No More: Prophecy Belief in Modern American Culture.* Cambridge, MA: Harvard University Press, 1994, p. 73.

45. Quoted in Archiving Early America, "Declaration of Independence." www.earlyamerica.com/earlyamerica/freedom/doi/text.html.

46. Jim Peterson, "The Revolution of Belief," Early American History message board, 2007. www.earlyamericanhistory.net/founding_fathers.htm.

47. Will Durant, *The Age of Voltaire.* New York: MJF, 1997, p. 121.

48. Thomas Jefferson, "Writings of Thomas Jefferson," Classical Liberals. http://classicliberal.tripod.com/jefferson.

49. Quoted in U.S. Constitution Online, "The United States Constitution." www.usconstitution.net/const.html#am1.

50. Butler, *New World Faiths.* pp. 132–133.

51. Quoted in Hunter Miller, ed., *Treaties and Other International Acts of the United States of America.* vol. 2, docs. 1–40:1776–1818. Washington, D.C.: Government Printing Office, 1931. http://avalon.law.yale.edu/18th_century/bar1796t.asp#art11.

52. Butler, *New World Faiths.* pp. 148–149.

Time Line

1484

Pope Innocent VIII issues an edict saying that witches are real, contributing to an upsurge in witch hunts in Europe.

1561–1626

Life of Francis Bacon, an Enlightenment thinker who exerts a strong influence on religious and scientific thought in the American colonies.

1618–1648

The Thirty Years' War, fought between Protestants and Catholics, ravages Europe.

1636

The Puritans establish Harvard College in Massachusetts, in large part to train ministers.

1648

Shah Jahan, emperor of India, erects the magnificent Taj Mahal as a monument to his deceased wife.

1682

Quakers begin to settle in Pennsylvania.

1687

The first Anglican services take place in formerly all-Puritan Massachusetts.

1692

Twenty people are executed and hundreds jailed during witch trials held in Salem, Massachusetts.

1695

The first permanent Jewish synagogue in British America is built in New York City.

1701

The Anglican Church in London establishes an organization to promote its ministries in the American colonies.

1706–1790

Life of Benjamin Franklin, a deist and one of the chief colonial American exponents of the Enlightenment.

1721

Puritan minister Cotton Mather publishes *The Christian Philosopher*, which reconciles religion and science.

1734–1744

Years of the great awakening, an upsurge in evangelical preaching and churchgoing in the colonies.

1741

George Frideric Handel composes the famous choral work *The Messiah*.

1761

Rumors spread that the Anglicans are scheming to install a bishop in the American colonies.

1762

Catherine II (the Great) becomes ruler of Russia.

1776

The American colonies separate from the mother country, creating the United States; a Connecticut minister announces that Jesus Christ's second coming is imminent.

1786

Virginia passes a statute of religious freedom, penned by Thomas Jefferson.

1787

The founding fathers begin to draft the U.S. Constitution, which comes to guarantee religious freedom and separation of church and state.

For More Information

Books

Patricia U. Bonomi, *Under the Cope of Heaven: Religion, Society, and Politics in Colonial America.* New York: Oxford University Press, 2003. This is a detailed, widely acclaimed examination of the various ways that religion affected colonial American society.

Paul Boyer and Stephen Nissenbaum, *Salem Possessed: The Social Origins of Witchcraft.* Cambridge, MA: Harvard University Press, 1974. Many historians consider this to be the most important recent study of the reasons for the witchcraft hysteria in Salem, Massachusetts.

Jon Butler, *New World Faiths: Religion in Colonial America.* New York: Oxford University Press, 2007. This is an important new study of religion in colonial America, with examinations of Native Americans, African slaves, Jews, and other minority groups, as well as Protestants and Catholics.

Peter Farb, *Man's Rise to Civilization as Shown by the Indians of North America from Primeval Times to the Coming of the Industrial State.* New York: Penguin, 1991. This modern classic discusses Native American religious beliefs and ideas along with many other aspects of Indian culture.

Edwin S. Gaustad and Leigh E. Schmidt, *The Religious History of America.* San Francisco, CA: Harper, 2002. This book is a fine, general overview of the many religions that shaped early America.

Frances Hill, *A Delusion of Satan: The Full Story of the Salem Witch Trials.* New York: De Capo, 2002. This is a well-organized and well-written account of the Salem witch trials by one of the leading authorities on the subject.

Frederick E. Hoxie, ed., *Encyclopedia of North American Indians.* Boston, MA: Houghton Mifflin, 1996. This book offers a large, highly informative overview of the tribes, leaders, experiences, and religious beliefs of Native Americans.

James H. Hutson, *Religion and the Founding of the American Republic.* Washington, D.C.: Library of Congress, 1998. This book discusses the state of religious beliefs in late colonial America and the Revolutionary period in-depth.

Joel W. Martin, *The Land Looks After Us: A History of Native American Religion.* New York: Oxford University Press, 2001. This book provides much useful information about the many Indian faiths practiced in the Americas during the era of white settlement.

John C. Miller, *The First Frontier: Life in Colonial America.* Lanham, MD: University Press of America, 1986. A very thoughtful and useful look at life and customs in colonial America, this book features numerous colorful primary source quotations.

Alan Taylor, *American Colonies: The Settling of North America*. New York: Penguin, 2001. This is an extremely well-researched and nearly definitive treatment of the subject by a Pulitzer Prize–winning scholar.

Louis B. Wright, *The Cultural Life of the American Colonies, 1607–1763*. New York: Harper and Row, 2002. This classic volume includes some information about colonial religions, along with studies of education, drama, music, and more.

———, *Everyday Life in Colonial America*. New York: Putnam's, 1965. Although an older work, this study of the subject by a leading scholar in the field remains one of the best. Contains a chapter on colonial religious beliefs.

Web Sites

Early Americas Digital Archive (www.mith2.umd.edu/eada). A collection of contemporary writings from colonial America.

Famous Trials (www.law.umkc.edu/faculty/projects/ftrials/ftrials.htm). Contains several accounts from the famous Salem witch trials.

Kidipede (www.historyforkids.org/learn/northamerica/after1500/religion/quakers.htm). An informative overview of the Quakers in colonial times.

Sage History (www.sagehistory.net/colonial/docs/winthrop.htm). Contains John Winthrop's well-known Model of Christian Charity speech.

Index

Picture Credits

About the Author

Historian and award-winning author Don Nardo has written many books for young adults about American history, including *The Salem Witch Trials*, *The Sons of Liberty*, *The Declaration of Independence*, *The Mexican-American War*, *The Great Depression*; biographies of presidents Thomas Jefferson, Andrew Johnson, and Franklin D. Roosevelt; several volumes about Native American history and culture; and a survey of the weapons and tactics of the American Revolution. Nardo lives with his wife, Christine, in Massachusetts.